A Story of Adoption

Saving Grace

L.B. JOHNSON

outskirtspress

DENVER, COLORADO

Outskirts Press, Inc.
http://www.outskirtspress.com

ISBN: 978-1-4787-5414-5

Outskirts Press and the "OP" logo are trademarks belonging to Outskirts Press, Inc.

PRINTED IN THE UNITED STATES OF AMERICA

For the Henley Family – Dan, Joy, Elisabeth, Faith, and Veronica. For being the face and faith of the adoption process.

Table of Contents

1

A Photo on a Dashboard

She would not have noticed the town that first time but for the speed trap. It was a two-lane shortcut to the interstate heading north, a sign that says 50 mph and then almost immediately afterward one that says 35 mph, as the first building just seems to pop up from the flat landscape like a diorama. It's not a route she normally drove, but with an accident backing up the freeway around the city this made for a good detour.

There are only a few buildings: a church, a small fire station, a half dozen very old homes; a couple of them kept in pristine condition, the rest having given up on curb appeal. There's not much in the way of business, though at some point this town was a small hub of activity in this land that was more farm than subdivisions. There's a pizza store and two antique-craft kind of places, colorful wares on display in the hopes that someone will make a stop.

Normally she would enjoy such places, appreciating the work of things made with one's own hands, the patina that is polished wood. But one of these is now closed, replaced by a store that sells decorative yard things, all cheap and likely made in China; the other with a *Closed* sign that only draws in the dust. Given the severe cold this winter, what little business they had has likely stayed indoors.

Today is no different. The air is cold. Clear. Sharp. Cutting like a knife to the landscape, flayed and laid bare to the eye under the surgical light of a winter morning. It's hard to believe that just 5 miles south is a bustling community of subdivisions and quickly constructed strip malls. On this road, in the hesitation that is the slow passage through this community, it could easily be seventy-five years ago; the structures unchanged, only more weathered. Behind are fields that clutch onto the skeletons of crops that died long ago, miles of bare windswept trees and clusters of burrs that stick to everything with a tiny pinprick of pain. It's a once pretty place that is clinging to the landscape as hard as it can, soon to be pulled free with that final stab of cold hurt.

At ten below with wind chill and an obligation to keep, it's another day when she does not stop. The fact is not lost on her that it's yet another nail in the coffin of what is left of those businesses.

The cold restricts movement as it propels it, pushing us toward something that will warm us. The cold, like life, only accentuating that which we cannot sustain. You move forward, or you will die.

Given the amount of traffic on this road and the widening of it further on, it's not hard to imagine that soon this town will be gone. The majority of the few buildings are close to the road, except for the church and a couple of homes with a large yard between house and road. The widening of the road to four lanes will be their inevitable end. The *For Sale* signs on the remaining well-kept houses are a literal sign, not just a physical one, of the town not having a failure but a mutiny. The few other houses look as if they are just waiting for someone to show up with a check and a bulldozer, if not abandoned already; sidewalks raised and broken; trash gathering in the cracks like autumn leaves; an old car in a yard, abandoned like a ghost ship.

As she passes that last *For Sale* sign she can't imagine selling her home, knowing that it will be razed. Even harder is having to walk away from it simply to save your life.

She had married too young into a Southern family who considered themselves as such, even though they lived in what the rest of the country considered the Midwest. It depends on which direction you looked at things, she reckoned; our individual horizons incised in whetted contrast to the circumference of this flat, harsh landscape.

Weather wasn't the only thing that was new to her, coming here from out West. But it was what she learned, and quickly. She learned what was safe to stay out in and what was not, learning early we are just pawns of the elements; severe weather usually arriving in the late hours like a black knight, rushing in, ready to do battle with the sleeping.

The family had a few hardscrabble acres on which rocks were the preferred crop, as well as a growing herd of cattle. It was a small farm, one which wouldn't have sustained them had she not held other jobs. Friends would tell her how lucky she was to have the land and the freedom; and she was. But she realized that in actuality it was like having two full-time jobs, seven days a week. Add to that family, dogs, cats, and a husband on a medical discharge from the military battling his demons, and she couldn't remember a day from that time when she just wasn't tired.

Twenty years in the future, she'll hear the radio announcer come on with a "Remember this classic from the '80s?" She'll turn the volume up to listen. And she doesn't. Remember. Those years to her were sweat and work, the smell of cow manure, propane, and the salt of tears; moments of roses and moments of thorns being of equal duration, passing too quickly in recollection. Looking in the mirror she sees the small lines that indicate her age—but she doesn't feel it. It's as if those entire ten years happened to someone else; endless alternating days and nights like a vacuum in which no air would come.

Given the choice, would she have taken that time back? Perhaps not. We do not cease from our experiences; in the end we arrive back where we started, seeing our struggles as if for the first time, but at a nice safe distance with wisdom otherwise not gained. This was a time to grow, to learn, to build. She learned how to fix a furnace and pull a calf from its mother; how to make supper out of almost nothing, the household money squandered on chasing something no one could provide even as she pulled down her shirtsleeves to hide the bruises. She learned how to hold her head up high in a small town buzzing over the gossip that came with that. And she learned to walk away when the demons finally won.

She recalls one of the last nights there, the brand of coat and boots she wears today no different than the ones she looked for that night as the glare of the headlights illuminated the room. It was a cattle truck coming at night so as to reach the stock-yards in the morning. She had woken alone to the rattle coming up the road. Trying to get a little nap before they arrived, springing like a bow from her bed, aware of her responsibilities. As she donned work clothes and boots, the orange running lights and diesel growl outside of the window reminded her of Martians landing, searching the house for signs of human life; and the first smile in a long time passed her lips.

All they would find was a lone woman, with boots, a shotgun she knew how to use, and a kitchen that once had smelled of cinnamon.

The driver backed around, turning the trailer with a gentle sigh of air brakes up to the wooden chute there at the barn. Within came the muffled grunt of the cattle that were being sold. Besides the lumbering truck and its driver and the cattle, she was alone. No cars, no help, the Earth hanging suspended in space, cooling, wearing only a thin veil of wood smoke. The wind cut her face, a blade that only stroked the skin, not cutting it, her hands aching as she rubbed them on her thighs, trying to stir warmth back into dormant skin.

Oh, how she longed to just go back to bed, the rustle of cotton, the panting whisper of breath, the predation of the night assuming a hundred avatars of dreams. No cows, no work, simply the house still and quiet as if marooned in space by the dwindling of day. The truck long gone, the sounds outside fell to a low fragmentary pitch. A coyote's howl at the indignation of clouds that covered the moon; no other sound made. Prey gone into hiding, insects dead with cold, everything else assuming their own mantle of hibernation or hunt.

But there was work to be done.

Hooves rattled in the trailer as it rocked and swayed, cattle moving with the chaos of their own confusion. All that was left was one lone cow, a young heifer that would go to a neighbor's farm for breeding stock. She stood forlorn in the fog of her own shadow, form turning as insubstantial as mist. The cow gazed at her as if she knew what was happening, looking at her with the obtrusive countenance of a stone god before turning and vanishing into space.

It was hard to decide which ones to keep and which to let go. Love, life, and longing, a helix viewed by eyes that see with hesitant, hungry fire. Decisions. They took from the land that which they needed to survive, giving something back; yet there was still in her that sense of loss even as she knew it was unavoidable, as are so many inevitable things.

The cattle truck's door closed with a profound finality, isolating them, isolating her as she watched it drive off. All that remained was to go back into an empty house to curl up in the guest room, the neatly made bed in the master bedroom a paradox within four walls redolent of long-abandoned warmth.

The land went to his family, their little farmhouse to be sold, tools replaced by others which would draw their own blood as she learned to live again amidst hard work, but work that was her calling. She couldn't bear to watch as the house was cleaned and made ready for sale, sun shining in on polished floors as undisturbed as frigid pools underneath the overhanging branches of shrouded furniture. When she left that night, she took just one thing with her, to carry in her vehicle as a reminder.

⬥⬥⬥

She still works too often out in the cold, and there are many nights when she gets only a few hours of sleep before going back on duty, watching the world come into a caffeine-induced clarity that does not bode well for the Sandman. Nights where she's not woken by the sound of cattle trucks, but by a phone, a voice on the other end speaking with an impersonal dry cadence she knows is more protection than uncaring; and she must quickly pull herself from bed, gathering a black bag and some gear, limbs wooden with the regret of lost slumber.

Sometimes she comes home and simply drops her clothes at the door, too exhausted to put them in the laundry. Pouring a finger of whiskey in a glass and flinging it back with a gesture that puts behind her all the suffering she has seen, tossing it back and away, leaving only the taste of smoke on her tongue, a scent that clings to her even after she sheds her clothes.

It's not always an easy life, but it's a good life, she thinks as that dwindling town fades from her rear-view mirror, her vehicle moving toward tenacious clusters of farms strung along a lonely river. Old barns listing and tumbling down, gone the way of the ancestors who built them long ago, going West, to dust. The clouds move so quickly she can't catch them with a fast car, grass laid flat in submission. Even the wind turbines seem to lean forward, waving their arms as if losing balance before a fall. A cold front has passed, the wind is howling, isobars dancing cheek to cheek as they move across the map to the Northeast. Despite the cold, she glances at her reflection in the mirror and sees a smile. Endings are always beginnings, even as the wind blows.

She is glad she came here to this place, so different from that first ramshackle country home and the large showpiece she bought later after years of hardship, as if by adding things to your life you can somehow make up for what was taken away. She'd sold that place at a loss and given away most of her possessions, understanding after the years alone what made her happy; and it wasn't things nor the type of people to which that mattered.

Before she gets to the freeway she crosses what was once an old wagon trail, families heading from the East to further west, to more open land and bigger homesteads. There's not much to mark those passages except for an occasional historical sign somewhere. But underneath the soil are the remains of all that did not finish the journey. The plains are dotted with the slumbering bones of cherished belongings, left behind to lighten the load to get through the hills further west; offloaded despite the tears of a woman to ensure the travelers would reach their destination. Furniture crafted by sweat and time; an upright piano left on a low rise by the trail, hopefully to be picked up by someone before it was forever silent.

Elsewhere, there are the graves: a young woman who didn't survive childbirth on the trail; the very old or the very young, felled by a simple virus or bacteria that prey on those who go hungry too often. Some of those graves are marked with only a cross, perhaps a young woman's name, a lock of her hair, and her wedding dress the only things that will see the Western sunset up close, the red sky curling up like shavings of wood that formed her grave marker.

There are dozens of graves like this on the wagon trails, some hidden in plain sight, others to be unearthed only when the earth itself is torn asunder. Nothing is left but some stones, or for a few a wooden cross, the gloss of light on its surface and shapes of long forgotten shadows on its bark. And with those solitary crosses are the remains of household goods, items too big or too cumbersome to take the rest of the journey, whatever joy and memory they held. Some pieces end up in museums, not looking as battered as you would expect as others came and collected them. They appeared almost as if they knew their role in the scheme in things, and their place was just where they ended, their destiny to be left waiting patiently in the tracks of the wagon until someone recognized their worth and laid claim to them.

On the way back from work that night she stops in that little town—but the businesses are all closed, the places silent. From a tree comes the sound of a single mourning dove, the note falling like liquid, taking shape as it descends through the frigid air, only to shatter as it hits unyielding ground. As she walks back to her vehicle in the frozen silence, she has a feeling that come spring she would drive here to find the road closed, machinery already tearing up the earth, disturbing the burial site of many a memory. She hopes those who lived away from the road could adjust to the noise; those who lived where the road would lie might find a new path.

Sometimes you make the decision, sometimes it's made for you. How you respond lies in what you need and the compromises with which you can live. You take what remains that brings you joy and you move forward, she thinks as she pulls her coat closer around her. The winds from the West still blow on the prairies, wailing a hymn of our mortality. Our remoteness stands watch over a fragility that is further honed by solitude. Yet in this season between hope of rain and hard winter comes peace—even as outside the air stills with a windless cold that only heightens her heart's heat.

As she turns back onto the two-lane highway, she notices that the trees branches are glazed with frost. Each branch shimmers in the fading light, as unique as it is alone. When people first settled this part of the country, their homes were built from these old trees and what precious nails they could spare, doing what they could to survive with what they had. Sometimes the very things that drew them here drove them away. Then they would move on, but not before burning their own homes to reclaim the nails that had held them together.

She drives away, a darkened and weathered nail hanging by a slender cord from the radio dial, next to a well-worn picture of a baby, faded by the sun, stained by tears.

2

Lessons from the Road

This is her story, it is my story, but where it began was so long before that long drive to a new life--it's one I can look back on now, another lifetime later. That little baby picture? I still carry it in my wallet, but it lies next to another: a young woman with flaming red hair like mine, with two babies beside her. They only exist because of *this* story: one of my brother Allen and me and how we came into a family.

I thought of him tonight as I drove to a work assignment, some-place out where it was cold and barren but for some emergency vehicles waiting for me. I no longer live out West, but with my husband in a tidy little bungalow closer to the Windy City, a place where weather can be just as treacherous. We're newly-weds, my getting the courage to remarry after twenty years on my own, with an introduction by friends and a bit of help from a big black dog. But that is its own story.

When the visibility is down around a quarter of a mile, that truck in front of me seems no larger than a spool of thread un-til its brake lights come on, and then it looks enormous. With almost a foot of snow it looks so peaceful out there, everything blanketed in white, as innocent and smooth as the surface of so much cream. But it's not a good day for travel; hundreds of flights canceled, probably thousands when all is said and done. Don't drive if you don't have to, the radio warns, as under the hood the engine rumbles with threat and promise both.

Allen, being my only sibling, had taught me how to drive; but what I remember most was his teaching me how to drive in the snow out in the West where we grew up, the two of us and our parents. We'd take the little VW Bug I had over to the empty high school parking lot where there were no people or light poles. There I learned all about braking, sliding, skidding, and the physics of stopping with a stalemate of snow and rubber. He'd teach me to recognize a skid, how to immediately pick out a distant visual target and keep your eyes *focused on that target,* while I steered out of it as he issued commands to keep me pointed in the right direction like a border collie directs cattle—his tone fast and quick and light, words darting in and out of my field of vision.

As I relaxed into well-practiced maneuvers, I simply listened to him talk; about things that angered him, things he wished he could change as he got older, what was right with the world, and what he could to do preserve those things. And I quietly listened, there amidst snow flying as if from a blower and do-nuts formed of chewed rubber, circles as identical and monoto-nous as milestones.

I put his teachings to test on hill and valley, letting that little car run like it was a horse, leaning forward with a yell as we got into fourth gear, as if by doing so I could somehow outpace it as we both fled the sheer inertia of Earth. That car and my spirit ran free of the fence lines, free of themselves, racing with a quality of movement in our motion totally separate from the imaginary pounding of hooves or the whoop of joy as I discovered flight in four-wheeled form. I put mile after mile on that car, the land stretching out until only darkness stopped her, the heavy scent of pines lying across the road for my trusty steed to disperse as if the scent were tangled skeins of smoke.

I also knew when to rein it in, slowing it down on slippery turns, downshifting through those sharp corners that are judgment and sentence and execution. I knew to stay behind the clusters of bright shiny cars, artificial flowers to which the restless bees of the law would be drawn. I also knew when to drive away, coasting out of a driveway when I arrived at a high school crush's to find him with someone else—that long slow tearing that leaves no scar of tire, only an internal lament that is the rending of raw silk.

Those lessons saved me more than once, like when the car slid toward an embankment late one night, that dark space where one's shadow waits for your death, only to recover and continue on. You've likely been there as well. It happens so fast: one minute you're staring bored at the speedometer, and the next you're snatched out of your lane in a torrent of rubber and refinanced steel, other vehicles scattering like rabbits suddenly looking for their warren.

When that happens you may not even know the cause--speed, black ice, or the force of Mother Nature that's as distant to indictment as God. All you know is that for a moment your useless hands are clasped tight to a useless steering wheel, and by only muscle memory you try and keep the pointy end forward, the headlights revealing not your safety but the now-empty road's abiding denial. When you finally stop all you can hear is your heart and the tick of a watch, that curved turmoil of faltering light and shadow in mathematical miniature reminding you how close you came to running out of time.

Such moments are the reason my last little car was traded in on a truck, though in city traffic a truck would be about as maneuverable as a dirigible. But I don't mind. I know about weather and idiot drivers, and I also know about fate. Because fate waits, needing neither patience nor appetite—for yesterday, today, and tomorrow are its own. For fate I'll arm myself, as I look down on a little Smart car scooting along the slick road between semis like a lone circus peanut among a herd of stampeding elephants.

I come to a halt at a rest stop. I get out, stomach in knots, regretting downing the salmon oil supplement with my vitamins and a glass of milk on an otherwise empty stomach. As I walk through the trees an unladylike belch sneaks out, fragrant with salmon— and I can only think to myself: I've survived the drive, now I'm going to get eaten by a bear in a rest stop in the middle of nowhere.

But I make it back to the vehicle with some animal crackers from a vending machine, none the worse for wear, hoping I can make it through the night without running off the road, wishing I had Allen with me for company.

I hear his voice in my head on that drive, echoes of the phone calls we made over the years. Sometimes he just wanted to vent a bit—not about the particulars of his military work, which he would never discuss—but simply other things he'd gone through. Our Mom's death to cancer when we were barely out of school; a fire that took his home; a bitter divorce. But I'd let him talk without interruption. For one thing he taught me other than slips and skids: that there are things we should never stop refusing to accept. Be it injustice and dishonor and outrage, not for cash for a better car, not for accolades, not for anything. There are things one must continue to be outraged over, to fight for, hands firmly on the wheel of where you want your life to go. His words are in my ears to this day: "You will have regrets, but never let yourself be shamed."

So many words of his as I drive along, words of not just wheels, but commitment to something bigger than both of us. They are words that got me to change course when I lost direction, words that helped me as well to take on a mantle of duty I never regretted even as I was forced to put it down; words to live that last life that I left behind. Now, years later, I have taken up that duty again, with his words—words that like a long climb up a rocky road were stepping stones of atonement. All of them words I'll remember long after he is gone, words that I've handled so long the edges are worn smooth; words that will keep me alive.

"Focus on the target, you can do this. . ."

3

Homecomings

Thinking of my brother comes naturally whenever I'm driving. Because the story of Allen and me began with a car ride, the first with our mom and dad.

Mom and Dad grew up in Montana, playing together as children, marrying as soon as Dad got home from serving in the 8th Air Force, stationed in Great Britain. The only reminders of that relationship I have left are letters and pictures, carefully packed in a trunk that lay in the attic until my brother and I liberated it.

There are so many photos of an 8th Air Force Liberator flying among flak as thick as snowflakes, soaring desolately above land whorled with unrest, the craft solitary above the destruction that it would rain. There underneath the photos lies a stack of letters. Mom and Dad wrote to one another for four years while he was overseas, not returning stateside once during that entire time. Reading them feels a little like eavesdropping, as you can almost hear the words as they formed—heartfelt, intimate. I opened one; it was just one single page, and I thought of the way their day stopped at the brink of it. In these letters bridging the time and distance they had to be apart, there was talk of how much they missed one another; of how their families were faring; of good coffee and how Dad missed vegetables from the farm; of burning heat and a cold on the field that would murmur to your very bones. There was playful affection, there was unstated passion and stated promise. Some was in Mom's flowery script, the rest in Dad's meticulous, indomitable hand. "Is everyone there well?" Mom would ask, and Dad would reply that they were (though some were now only well beyond Lamentations). "How is the homestead?" Dad would ask, and Mom would reply, "Fine," not telling him that they were occasionally going hungry.

They spoke of the future, of their past. They did not speak of the aircraft that limped back to England only to crash on approach, their violent end felt through the ground like a vibration rather than heard. They did not speak of her working two jobs after her dad's death while logging, to support two younger brothers and her mom. So much spoken and unspoken, like two mourning doves calling back and forth across an endless summer—all now just held together by a blue silk ribbon.

Not all missives that went back and forth over the seas were good news. Just up the road from Mom's, the week after Pearl Harbor a neighbor stood by the mailbox with a piece of paper not even big enough to start a fire with, the envelope fallen to the ground as bland words exploded one by one, and that family's grieving began. There was only the notice, there was nothing to bury—though you don't need a wooden box to capture the form of courage and sacrifice.

I wonder how many millions of messages like that went out in old wars, not taking long to read, as there was no real time in it; not in that demarcation between the hope that someone lived, and that place where you knew that was no longer true, when you wished that this moment existed only outside of time. There were only moments in which a written word hung in the air as if hopeful silence had been so long undisturbed that it had forgotten its purpose.

I look again at those letters Dad kept. The actual forming of the characters is uniform, flowing, like words pent up too long. The letters are sixty-some years old, powdery and delicate in my hand. But sixty years were just a moment ago for my dad, something as fierce and encompassing as war always standing out in his memory, no matter how many years distanced him from battle.

So he returned to her, they married, and my mom immediately became pregnant, only to go into labor many weeks too early. Their daughter lived only days, while Mom battled an infection that would leave her barren.

They were together, their dream for years. But although it was an abundant life—Mom working as a deputy sheriff, Dad getting his CPA license and finding a job with one of the big timber mills—their home was missing the sound of children.

So the long, sometimes painfully arduous process of adoption was begun. When it didn't happen immediately, they applied to be foster parents—however they could get a child in their home, just to hear a child's laughter. I don't have all the details, but Allen and I came into their lives when we were very young.

Mom and Dad had intended on getting just one child, but having completed the paperwork, when they heard there were two of us there was no real discussion, only logistics. For they only had a child seat for one, for the three hour drive home. My brother Allen, being the oldest, got the seat. They put me *in a box.*

Well, it *was* a large box, carefully padded with coats and a pillow, and lashed in tight to the back of the seat with a seat belt.

Still, years later I can hear my brother lean over with a grin on the retelling of that story with "They liked *me* better!" and how we would laugh.

We came home to a post-war subdivision, houses popping up starting in the late '40s, with new streets like ours hubbing off them in the 1960s as the town prospered and people expanded their families in a time of peace and abundance.

Dad still lives there all these years later. Going home now as an adult to visit him, I'm surprised how quiet it is outside; the kids all inside the local school, neighborhood moms and dads both working much of the time these days. Off in the distance, the wail of a police siren. The ground is hard and knotted; the houses stare silently forward, not acknowledging anything that exists in their peripheral vision. The morning light falls down upon their steps in silence. That lack of sound does not seem odd, it is simply winter.

Dad slumbering in the back room, tiring easily at age ninety-four, I sit in the chair by the picture window and look out at the same homes I saw as a child; and I think back to those glory days when Mom and Dad brought us home, how this whole neighborhood came alive. Mom's been gone many years; Dad outlived both her and my stepmom in this house. And although the family dynamic is different, the sounds of this home remain.

Especially during summer the neighborhood took on another depth of sound. There was the bright, disorderly cry of lawn-mowers firing up; the small tidy yards of an older neighborhood not taking all day to mow, but the precision of their care reflecting the owners' pride in their homes. There were no homeowners association rules. One neighbor's bright purple door stood out at attention, but with the colorful flowers that normally adorned the front and the deep rosy hue of the brick, the color suited the house. There were a couple of kids on bikes, zooming up and down the sidewalks as off in the distance their dog barked for their return. Far away the sound of church bells, there in the month of white lace and showers of rice, paced faithfully and serenely; like shafts of light among the soft green leaves, yellow butterflies dancing on the grass like flecks of sun;

The sounds would continue into evening: a summer shower off the lake releasing the scent of flowers into the damp air;

crickets sawing away in the grass with an intensity you could almost feel as a tickle on the skin. There was the wave of a neighbor as he brought in the paper; the clink of a couple of glasses of Kool-Aid, sweet like nectar on the porch.

There was no formal neighborhood watch here, but we did look out for one another. Our parents noticed when the newspapers piled up at someone's house and would check to make sure they were OK. They paid attention to a strange car parked on the street, a teenage boy just stopping to visit with the pretty teenage girl down the road.

They would know who had a new child by the toys that sprouted in the yard like colorful flowers. Our moms would trade recipes and gossip over a fence, finding out who had been ill, who might need help with a new baby. For this wasn't just a neighborhood, this was a community—neighbor helping neighbor, the kids welcome at pretty much any home, stopping in on someone's mom if we needed a drink or the use of the bathroom.

Now, a lifetime later, the houses are the same, but the neighborhood is not. I note the silent homes, a sign gone up for a quick sale, the owner having passed away; time consuming not just courage but muscle and bone until nothing is left but a frail form draped in a white sheet, like a piece of unused furniture. We don't notice the exact time of leaving but can't help but speak of the remains. I note one house in disrepair, empty, likely a foreclosure; a local factory's shutting down taking with it not just jobs but a lot of hope.

Ours was a good house to come home to, though; a place of refuge for two lost little birds.

As I sit in the quiet, a small sparrow blows onto the sill like a bright scrap of paper, his heart pumping in his throat faster than any pulse. He looks into the house, then away, then into the glass again as if listening, only to dart away as the clock chimes on the hour, then ceases. The chime fills the whole house. Perhaps it's just sound—or perhaps it's all time, grievance, and grief manifesting as sound for just one instant as planets and gears align. It's a moment wherein time seems to stop, the sparrow frozen on the sill. Only when that sound stops does time come to life, and by then the bird is gone.

The only sound now is that of breath and the tick of the old clock. I don't deliberately listen to it, the ticks seemingly beyond the realm of hearing; then in a moment, with that one tick your ears respond to, you are acutely aware of the long diminishing train of time you did not hear. How many ticks in this house in fifty years? How many after I am long gone? Yet I feel the presence of others that have lived here, for they perhaps aren't truly dead but simply were worn down by the minute clicking of small gears. The echo of those who sat in this room do not disturb me; they are part of this house. Just like the sound of wood, its creak one of murmuring bones; and the air that taps on ancient glass speaks of deep winds that witnessed more than time.

Dad resting quietly, I take a quick walk before making his dinner, after which we will call Allen to catch up before seeing him on the weekend. As the neighborhood ticks a slow and steady beat outside, there comes the rumbling of the trains, the tracks a half mile away carrying a sound on the air that is as comforting as childhood. I watch the movement that is static serenity and labored exhaust, a rhythmic *click-click* as it moves away through eternal trees, faded to thick sky, the train displacing air.

Shadows lengthening, I hurry back to the house. The tick of my watch and the sound of the train dissolve away as if running through another place, someplace far from where this life ended up. I approach the house I grew up in, the porch glistening with a sheen of ice, its empty lattice the front guard of circumstance waiting for summer flowerings.

I think of the inordinate ticks of chance it took to bring my brother and me to this home, through which we were so blessed to be here. In the air scented with trees I ascend the steps, clutching the old key to the back door, there on a little ring with a train etched on it. In the growing dark I don't really see it, but I feel it in my hand, clinging to that little anchor to a life lived here long ago—a life unexpected but as welcoming as home.

The house sighs as I open the door. I catch a glimpse of myself in the mirror, moving away from its reflection into the warmth, my form darting out of sight; the sound, *tick-tock-tick-tock*, a wisp of air that breathes life back into this home.

4

Adding Pepper

"So, when can we get a dog?"

Those are words that probably every parent on the planet has heard. My brother and I were no different, asking as soon as we'd played with the neighbor's dog.

My parent's budget was tight. Mom had quit her job when they adopted us. She'd also had some health issues, diagnosed with colon cancer when I was just shy of four years old. She survived the initial round of fighting that dreaded disease, but with a lasting impact on her health, now tiring easily and having a colostomy to contend with on a daily basis in addition to a house full of redheads.

"*Please?*" Our parents heard it every day. We tried the logical pleas:

(1) It will scare off bears! (Not that I'd ever seen a bear around, just an occasional elk—most of whom were middle-aged men that met at the lodge and liked to golf.)

(2) It will provide Mom with company in the house when we start school. (As would soap operas, with much less dog hair.)

And the last one—what every parent since ancient Greece has heard:

(3) All the other kids have one! (Which was met with the same expression as if we'd said, "But *all* the kids have a flamethrower!")

There weren't any pet stores back in that day, at least not in our tiny little town. There were a couple of reputable hunting dog breeders, popular in all parts of the country. But those dogs were not an expense my parents could justify. Mom and Dad said they'd look in the paper to see if anyone had some pups for sale.

We ended up with a dog from the pound, a little female wiener dog mix we named Pepper. We're not sure where she came from originally; she wasn't a puppy when we first brought her home, but she was still young.

But my brother Allen and I had picked her out, as our parents had chosen us. Allen and I loved being her dog mom and dad, even though she viewed us as her pups. Pepper would patrol the hall outside our rooms at night with a click of little toenails on the hardwood, bark at the mailman, and beg us to let her out as if to say:

"Look out in the yard—squirrels! They're like tennis balls thrown by God!"

Wherever we went, she went; except to church and school, when she would patiently have to wait for us to come home.

Mom and Dad had her spayed so there wouldn't be any puppies; they explained there were so many unwanted animals in the world, it was best that folks gave some of those dogs a home first.

Pepper went with us everywhere, even on trips to Dairy Queen. When the weather got hot Mom would close up the drapes, turn on a fan, and try not to use the oven. Dinner was usually grilled, or a plate of cold meats and cheese, flatbread, and a glass of wine or beer for the adults, Kool-Aid for the kids. But if we were lucky we'd leave the house and head to Dairy Queen. Other than the McDonald's and the A&W Root Beer Drive-In, Dairy Queen was the only fast food in town.

I remember those trips: sitting in the car, also with no air conditioning, trying to eat the cone before the ice cream melted and ran down my shirt. Pepper even got her own serving, which Mom would patiently hold while Pepper lapped at it, crunching the cone like it was the world's best bone. Days of heat and glory. For a moment it wasn't hot; there was just the clear cold of the ice cream, eaten in hurried silence with the people we loved, cool salvation taken from summer's scorn.

We didn't have a mall; we hung around the water, near low-hanging rock ledges that we would jump off, by streams in which you could paddle around like in a preschool kiddie pool. The older kids, the braver ones, would jump off the higher rocks or grab an inner tube and propel themselves down through some rushing water to a pool further down, while the dog would just bark from all the excitement.

I remember hesitating to take that first leap into the abyss— until some older kid double dog dared me, and I raised an invisible fist to the sky in defiance of gravity and went over the edge. For a moment I thought Pepper was going to jump in with me—but when I popped to the surface I could just see her little head peering over the edge with an expression that said, "My humans, they are idiots!"

At home, there was a sprinkler or even a Slip'N Slide, where with a deep springing run you could launch onto a wet plastic superhighway off into the grass. "Geronimo! Wheee! DOG POOOOOP!"

We're not sure who rescued who there in those glory days, but we had found a new best friend.

5

On Being Special

I think I was about six when our parents explained the whole adoption thing, so we would understand before other children in school said something. As children the whole societal concept of family was almost foreign. Everything we knew was what had been experienced. That probably explained the fuss one day in Bible school when the teacher was talking about Adam and Eve's sons Cain and Abel. The story talks about Cain meeting his wife and begetting various children. Having no knowledge of such things, but understanding the concept that Adam and Eve were *it* as far as people on the planet, I raised *that* question, heard round the church: "Where did Mrs. Cain come from—was she his sister?"

I don't remember exactly how that was explained, but I remember my Sunday school teacher doing a "facepalm" when she heard the question.

So my parents did try to explain the whole dynamics of our coming to live with them. They sugarcoated it as best as they could, not telling me until later that I had screamed if anyone tried to touch me—and I mean *screamed* at the slightest touch; and Allen would rhythmically bump his head on his sleeper bed to the point they had to pad it. Apparently we came with some "issues." I don't recall them, and from what we were told later they were very short-lived. Once we knew we were safe, that was all we needed to know—and the rest faded to memories never retold.

We took the news quite well. We didn't grow in Mom's tummy like some of the other babies on the block, and they picked us out from a bunch of children, so we were *special*. With that we raced out into the back yard to play, darting in and around the clothesline like cattle dogs on caffeine.

That was our world: a family, a house, and always in summer those clothes hanging on the line.

As an adult now I still have a clothesline, and not because I can't afford a dryer. For to pull in a big batch of sheets from the line, kissed by the sun with the warm scent of summer on them, there is no fabric softener scent that can match that. There's something quietly satisfying about taking things that are dirty, the clothing of the people you love, and rendering them clean; a ritual of care that some folks would probably not understand. ("You *like* doing your husband's laundry?") But holding the clothing of those you love, something that bears their scent, their labors, and then carefully getting it ready for them to wear again has an intimacy of its own.

Growing up we always had a dryer, an avocado green Maytag.

But in the spring and summer Mom invariably hung the clothes outside. I have vivid memories of those days. I would help gather the clothes in, that being one of my set chores. For we had assigned chores as children, daily ones that had to be done without fussing if we hoped to get an allowance to buy us a bit of candy on Saturday. No chores, no allowance—that became obvious early. We were given things to do that were in the scope of our abilities, and some that were beyond, with supervision only when necessary so that we would learn, painfully if we didn't listen, but learn nonetheless.

The clothes would hang with the linens, dresses, and dress shirts; the modest nightwear; the men's briefs; and the big granny panties that we wore, ones that did not peek out of low slung jeans but only the Sears Catalog. There was our Sunday best, to be appropriately scratchy for young ones in the pew to squirm around, while Pastor Erickson talked of Genesis and Exodus and fathers therein who dared the joy to talk face-to-face with God.

On laundry day, when the clothes were off the line to be taken inside and sorted, Mom would set up the ironing board in front of the TV. There she would watch *As the World Turns*, *The Secret Storm*, or *Guiding Light* while she ironed and I put together the puzzles that fascinated me, Allen off at school. To this day Dad still has a jigsaw puzzle of bears on the coffee table that was purchased for my brother, not that it stopped me from putting it together time and time again until the edges were worn.

While I played Mom would iron everything, including the

sheets; from the hand-embroidered ones of the '50s to the harvest gold striped ones from the late '60s and '70s. She'd use a wine bottle with a cap that allowed for water to be sprinkled out in lieu of a steam iron, as if subtly blessing the sheets. There was an almost Zen-like ritual to it, a series of defined movements done in proper order with the right amount of physical force and the elements that comprise the process.

Then she would get the after-school snack out and dinner prepared, giving her just enough time to freshen up and make a martini to greet my Dad at the door when he got home. Lest you think my Mom a demure Mrs. Cleaver type: prior to adopting us, when she wasn't doing laundry she was the county sheriff. College educated when most women didn't get past high school, Mom could kick butt and take names, help pluck out a drowning victim from the river, and deal with the trauma that was rape, domestic violence, and abuse.

I'm sure she missed the challenges, but after eighteen years as a law enforcement officer Mom found greater satisfaction in maintaining order in a house of redheads and occasionally fishing someone's toy out of the toilet. Everything she did she did with care and attention to detail, even in the later years when cancer called for her.

I still remember the days when Mom washed my stuffed animals and carefully hung them up by the ears on the clothesline, giving each one a little kiss and a pat while I watched to make sure they were OK. One of them had one eye and little fur, he being loved so hard, but she very carefully hung him up by the ears with a special kiss. I thought he had disappeared; but when she was in her last days and I was leaping into adulthood, she put him away where I'd find him again when I was grown, to remember those days.

I remember her as well, dealing with Allen and Dad's filthy and smelly fishing garb, simply smiling gently and handling them as delicately as vestments. She worked away, a patient smile on her face, the birds on the power lines and in the trees singing a hymn of praise as she labored for love.

While the clothes fluttered on the summer line like the last valiant leaves of the year, we'd run and play. If we fell down, we got up; if we skinned a knee, we washed it off with the hose; running in and out of the hanging sheets, bright red heads flashing through them like birds. We did so with a zest for breathing that is wrung out of most people by the time they're forty, playing as if we were eternal—and in that moment we were, there in the clean open air away from the walls of dust and shadow and sickness.

Allen and I played hide-and-seek and cowboys and Indians. We stalked squirrels and each other with nothing more than a plastic weapon and iron courage. Our games had elements of make-believe, of magic and superpowers, soldiers, secret agents, and spies. But we weren't so sheltered from the world to be unaware that being careless with the tools and talents we were given was to meet up with a beast that, though lightly slumbering, sleeps with blood-tainted breath. As we grew, we watched as deer fell in the woods under our guns, a firearm being more than a toy to play cops and robbers with: the means of putting food on the table, a means to protect, one that came with heavy responsibility.

We understood early on that some things do *not* wash out.

The clothesline eventually came down; I don't actually recall when. It was about the time Allen went off to the Navy, to submarine school. I wanted to go with him, as we did everything together; but I had a couple of years of school left. All I could do was stand there as a line that no longer held his shirts stood like a barren flag pole, and the vehicle in which we'd had so many adventures drove off toward his future. I watched as long and as hard as I could, thinking that old blue panel van would turn around. But the red taillights just got further away and closer and closer together, until my last memory was a small single spot of red that made my eyes weep as if I had dared to stare into the sun.

Things change, processes evolve, how we live, and where we live. But some things, the good things, could continue; and I didn't care if they are considered tacky or old-fashioned, they are a ritual of love that goes beyond blood and care that goes beyond obligation. Like my clothesline. The clothes are different: there are more T-shirts than dresses, a lot of khaki and navy and black. Some of the shirts have pictures; some just have big letters on them. There's the plaid flannel nightie for when it's really cold; but most of the underwear, if they were made of paper not fabric, wouldn't be big enough to start a fire with. Styles have changed, but some rituals haven't.

As I hang up a button-down dress shirt here in my home today, I think back to those long-ago days of my childhood when Mom did the same things for those she loved. She could have had a clothes dryer and not done all the work. She could have kept her home clean and pristine going into middle age instead of taking in two rambunctious kids at a time when her friends were becoming grandparents.

But she didn't—because we weren't the special ones, she was.

6

The Bicycle

As a child, I could never figure out why we got out of school in June. In the month of June it was still chilly on some mornings, rainy on others. Then, to add insult to injury, we had to go back the first part of September when the air was a fine golden wine that invited laughter and the shedding of long pants and shirts, as we got into trouble as only the innocent can down at the swimming hole.

But like kids do, we'd take in every last second—swimming, jumping from a rope swing into clear waters, ripping through the woods seeking things we thought were ours alone to discover. An old scrape of an antler, the footprint of a stealth fox, the glimmer of red the only sign that she had passed.

It was a rare day in summer where we'd stay indoors, and most of that time outdoors I was on my bike. My toys were beloved, but I *loved* my bike. However, I wanted a new one, specifically a ten-speed, when all the cool kids were getting $100 Schwinn bicycles. Dad's income was modest, providing simply a roof over our head, seed for the garden, and a steer to butcher each year; plus tithing for the church, and gas to go visit my aunt and uncle's house or a cabin at the coast for a few weeks each summer. We weren't lacking in a good, sound, loving home and physical comfort, but a $100 bike back in the late '60s was out of the question.

I was crushed, praying for what I wanted, not needed, as some people did, as if God was some sort of celestial room service. Yes, I prayed for a shiny yellow Schwinn. It was not to be, and knowing how hard my parents worked I tried not to let my disappointment show.

But I'd watch the other kids from up the ridge in the big houses of cedar and glass, whizzing down the hills on their brand new bikes. It wasn't jealousy so much as it was like looking through the telescope we'd watch the stars with, the lens tempting us with places we wished to go, places our senses could see but which our limitations could not afford.

I didn't whine, I didn't beg. That may have worked with the whole "get a dog" thing, but the dog was from the pound while a bicycle cost money. I rode the heck out of my old one-speed bike, hoping that *if* one day it would sort of spontaneously combust from that bump catapulting me downhill toward the grade school at Warp Factor 4, my parents would be *forced* to buy me a new one. But it didn't happen—neither the combustion, Warp Factor 4, *nor* the new bike.

Then, one hot late summer day Dad got up early. He normally rose before the sun, but this day he was up *really* early. When he came home he bustled something covered with a tarp into the garage and told us kindly but firmly to stay out. We figured it was woodworking stuff, a hobby he loved; and that was that.

Then we headed out into the fields, the kids from the hill where the big houses were on their new bikes, while I rode the dilapidated embarrassment of a little girl's bike complete with the hated basket. I wanted a big kid's bike, a cool bike. I was almost ten! But my parents knew better than to give us everything we wanted when we asked for it, so we would not grow up into that sense of entitlement that can only lead to disaster—as individuals, as a nation.

But cool bike or not, I loved to ride; and we'd race the wind, abandoned to the musical cadence of foot and spoke and pavement. The streets attested to the power of this freedom, kids racing up and down with war cries and laughter. Seeking out friends, seeking out adventures. Especially if it took us out into the woods that surrounded our little mountain town.

The bikes got us to this place, but it was always ours. Clear blue streams gurgling with trout, flotillas of the first yellow leaves rushing on and gathering in clusters against the rocks. We'd race down the hills on our bikes, shouting over the galloping hooves of our imaginary steeds. A hawk dove from the sky; the wilderness was his home, but it was ours to claim.

We'd drink from a clear mountain stream if we got thirsty, and we ripped more than one set of knees out of a pair of jeans which our mothers would patch, not replace. Our moms were all at home doing what moms secretly did in the day. My own, having been a sheriff in an adjoining big county, was high up on the Cool Chart, as was my dad; but we never felt tethered by them, only protected. They trusted us to travel in pairs, to wander in by dinner, and to come home if anyone accidentally lost a limb or caught a really big trout.

They seemed to understand that we needed to burn off the energy of youth and growth. They knew who we were with and likely where we would be; but they allowed us to work through the precursors of teen hormones, exploring, building a raft, not cooped up inside. They had grown up with this generation of play, and so would we.

Our toy soldiers clashed and died while we, as general or spy, ran between the thick green trees until twilight rolled over us in clean, warm waves. Then with only the impending darkness and an empty belly we were called home.

We'd gather our wounded to us: the GI Joe that lost his arm in a tragic lumberjack accident; the precision plastic firearm that only dribbled water now; and field nurse Barbie who never had the appropriate outfit. Our next-door neighbor boy Craig with his skinned knee and my brother Allen with his sunburn retreated to their bikes, which they rode together as best friends for the next fifty years.

School was almost upon us, and every last bit of adventure was squeezed from the day before we arrived back home. We crept into the pantry, grabbing a Hostess Sno Ball from the cupboard, and then rushed out to see what Dad was doing, cheeks stuffed with chocolate and marshmallow like wild-eyed squirrels. There was my dad. Not angry that we were dirty, with torn pants, and having a snack before Mom's homemade supper, but smiling. Beaming, actually. And there behind him was a ten-speed bicycle. Not a Schwinn. But a Huffy, repaired and freshly painted in my favorite color, with new decals and new tape on the handlebars.

"Would you like it?" he asked me with the hushed hesitation of that question where you knew before you asked what the answer would be.

At first I was astonished, not believing this was happening. Then the astonishment faded away, slowly at first, then evaporating quickly; and quietly, like a piece of iron being forged so hot that it glows, a glow sparked and then ebbed to the contentment of its final form, what it was destined to be.

Dad had gotten up at o'dark hundred hours to drive to the city where their police department was auctioning off unclaimed lost or stolen bikes to raise money for the community. He got up when some folks were going to bed and waited in the cold for hours to bid on this bike, which he got for $15, then repaired, painted and cleaned up. It wasn't new, but it gleamed with promise; the handlebars shone with invitation; and it was fast. Lord, it was *fast*.

My bike now is mostly a four-wheel-drive truck. I have one at work as well, to get to places people never want to go. The woods are still my second home, be it play or sometimes work, quiet bluffs and valleys that hide their dead. I may still come home dirty, and it's a frantic life some days; but being a grown-up doesn't mean we have to grow up, for we still wish for the same comforts and joys we experienced as children.

With my work today done, I head on north toward home. On the way, I take a side trip through a park and wildlife refuge; I roll down the window, feeling the cold air on my face as if riding my beloved bike. Then, from the woods as the light seeps from the sky, a form off in the distance. I slow and then stop in wonder. A large whitetail deer rushes from the trees; antlers held high, splashing over dappled current, then disappears without sound. His size and form leaving goosebumps on my skin, as if the departure of his presence blew hot and cold on me.

As I sit and watch him rush away I wonder where that old bike of mine ended up. Probably handed down to a niece or nephew, though neither of us could recall. But I will always remember the look on Dad's face when he wheeled it over to me and the feeling in me when I rode it for the first time, flying down our rural road—a fighter pilot of wheels and gears, my big brother riding close by as wingman.

In a few weeks, I think I need to go out to the garage. There is a bike there, the mountain variety, that's been harnessed too long. The sun is out, the roads are dry. If I look down I can see my face reflected in the polished handlebars—the face of a fighter, the scribe of rigid bone and the folly of men, overlaid with the wondrous childlike glee of unbound speed that knows not yet fate nor death.

I'm going to forget what the neighbors will think or how sore I might be later. I'm going to climb up on that bike as soon as I can and put that wind back in my wheels, the shadow of my wingman always behind me.

7

Taylor's Mountain

There is only one date on a child's calendar, and that is the first day of summer, that taste of hope and freedom long awaited.

Our hometown was at the base of mountains that I would not ascend for many years, our house in the slow rise up to the base, a valley of safe adventure. As kids we were not allowed up into the really steep hills, the roads there much too treacherous for bike and car to share. But oh, we would ride everywhere else. We'd play spy versus spy, soldiers, and cowboys, chasing each other all over the foothills and streets that had sprouted up around our place. I loved to ride my "new" bike. One can't help but be drawn in by the composition of the rhythm of leg and wheel; taking freedom from the movement, understanding without regret that it is only your effort that is making you fly. The harder you work, the further you'll go, determination outpacing antiquated spokes and wobbly tires, watching the world come into view and then passing away again.

The streets attested to the power of this drive, kids racing like kamikazes up and down driveways and over curbs with the requisite occasional crash and burn. We wore our bandaged knees like medals, for running home crying to Mommy would brand you a coward as quick as any action of your life. You held in your pain, and closeted it with the secrets you only told your best friend.

From the streets we'd head to the woods that rose like Oz from areas that had been cleared to put in the homes of the Baby Boomer generation. The bikes would be abandoned at the edge of our play. Crime didn't exist out here, at least not the kind that would regularly take some poor kid's bike, though it did happen once in a while. The bikes were abandoned, piled up like kindling wood, with nothing but footprints leading out into the trees. Out there in the wild we continued the games, screaming our lungs out with a war cry, chasing shadows as far as our legs could carry us. From the woods, the cry of a predatory bird challenging us. We'd stay out all day, a handful of cookies and some raisins stuffed into pockets, and consumed—smashed, gritty and sweet.

It was on those expeditions in an open track of land hidden by trees that we found it: our very own mountain. In a transitory, enchanted moment we held our breaths and slowly approached, the sun shining down as we approached with delighted awe that stirred like bees. It was a tall form of dirt and rocks, adventure as high up as we could climb. There were no adults to tell us to go home, no signs about trespassing. We left our bikes and made our way to the top, climbing over stone and scraggly plants, reaching the peak where we stopped to stare. There off in the distance, though we couldn't see our house, we could see our future; air rushing past us there in that new discovery, that still, fierce potency that satisfies hunger not yet known as desire.

We called it Taylor's Mountain.

We're not sure where the name came from. Perhaps we named it after the first kid who successfully got his bike to the top and rode it down without breaking a limb. I'm not even sure how long the mountain had been there, but we liked to believe we discovered it and soon laid claim to it. Scaling its height was anticipated glory, and we'd gather at its base after breakfast and move up and outward, a posse of potential.

We had no curfew. We played until the light waned and our stomachs told us it was near to supper time; and then we'd go home to the second best part of summer vacation, the family barbecue. Whether the food was perfect, burnt, or dried out, it was just *good* because it was made on the grill. It was made by *Dad*, and we got to eat it outside if we wanted. Afterward, if the night was clear, we'd pitch a pup tent in the backyard, pretending we were in the wilderness all by ourselves—and that Mom was not twenty yards away with cookies if we were hungry after fending off imaginary Indian raiders with our little six-shooters.

How well I remember those days—when the air was burning hot, the whiff of lighter fluid in the air, the dark nuggets of briquettes, overhead a badminton bird flying by the only sign of motion in the still summer air. Laughter as my brother and cousins played. Shadows on the grass as we ran and played under branches from which smoke drifted like a soft touch. Shadows that got to those trees before I did, then faltered, so I could stomp them into the grass under my bare feet.

The summer we found Taylor's Mountain was one that stands out. Not in the sense of the nostalgic, which holds with it some sense of time passing; a litany of hours of my time, my life, passing before my eyes in quiet dreams. It is distinct as if it stands with me here in these last few months where time slipped through my fingers like water, its quiet comfort and its loss felt on my hands in its very dissipation.

For there was more than smoke in the air that summer of Taylor's Mountain; something I was too young to understand but could sense. I was approaching the cusp of becoming a teenager; there was a war on; and I was becoming more aware each day that the world was changing around me. It was a different era than now. There were hippies and drugs and crime, yet somehow we were protected from the grown-up world. I didn't even know what sex was until I was twelve—and was ever so thankful I was adopted so my parents didn't have to do *that* (Dad about busted a gut laughing when I told him years later).

But we were allowed to be kids as long as our minds embraced the world with the wonder of childhood. As the world contemplated old disasters and future hopes, we were simply set free to be children. We wore no bicycle helmets; we drank from the garden hose; our mothers never organized a "play date," yet we made enough friends that we rarely came inside until the light had bled out of the sky. We'd run and we'd ride, calling loudly into the wind until the shouts of those years mounted toward a final crescendo, passing beyond the reach of hearing.

By day we'd ride to our mountain and conduct the warfare of youth, with squirt guns full of water from the hose, pine cone grenades, and sound effects that burst up out from our lungs, not some video game. We may have played life and death, but those afternoons were filled with time so solid we could have picked it up from the ground to place in our pocket with other treasures. Time so thick we could part it like a curtain, stepping into a dimension of imagination there on that tall, rock-diffused mass of earth, stepping onto mass that upheld us. We laughed on that mountain, and we bled from an assortment of childhood cuts and scrapes worn like badges of honor.

We played soldiers a lot. I was the recon team, moving fast, making no noise, not crying no matter what. Head down in leaves that smelled of old newspaper I tried not to think about my cousin, off at war; when he'd return from duty, when he'd pick me up and swing me around again, laughing. I only tried to be a stronger soldier, better, truer, to keep my men safe, to make him proud of me, even as they had declared a ceasefire upon discovery of a particularly large frog.

Time, dense and strong, would stop on those afternoons, was suspended as we only registered the sound of fake gunfire, the dog's bark, the artillery fire of a lawnmower. Then, only then, faint and insistent the call to home, the rumble of stomachs long past lunch.

There were days when due to hard rains or family activities we didn't get to the mountain for a few days, playing inside with model cars and Lionel trains instead until Mom called us to the family table for grace and pot roast. Nights when I'd politely ask to be excused as soon as I was done eating so I could go back outside, where I wanted to be despite the rain, a mist that had dampened that night's attempt to cook out. I'd walk down to the pond, stopping to stare into the water, down where I could see almost to the bottom, the last rays of sunlight playing like orange fire on the surface. There on the surface, a leaf. After a long time in water, the tissues of the leaf decayed, leaving only the fiber, swirling in the surface like soft bones, light from the last of the day's sunlight playing on them like flame. Summer was almost over, and soon Dad would be putting away the barbecue, just as we had to put away the bicycles before the first snow fell. I didn't want to come back into the house; I didn't want summer to end.

It was one of those sticky days in late August when the thought of another day of play was tickling my consciousness like a pilfered cookie. From my room I could hear the siren call of those last bronze days of summer, moving like music, flowing like honey in bright sunlight that danced against my window. It was time to seize the day as school was starting very soon. My mom would be up and there would be homemade bear claws, laughter, and the sun. Oh, the sun. Bright, trembling with the remnants of heat lying in open fields. The air lush with the smell of turning trees, blowing for a hundred yards against the vagrant air of summer vacation. It was an invitation no kid worth his salt could resist.

But Taylor's Mountain was not there. Over the weekend it had been torn apart by construction equipment. For Taylor's Mountain really wasn't a mountain: in anything other than the eyes of children it was merely a humongous pile of dirt and rock left some previous summer by a developer, only to have the subdivision plans go dormant in a time of war. But the economy was picking up, and the grounds of our play would be sacrificed to build homes for those returning. Taylor's Mountain was gone, but it was still within us—a form that uplifted us that glorious summer as we scrabbled over it, acting out our worries and our fantasies under the summer sun.

It's not what we've lost that matters, but what we find; each day of adventure we are granted. Days where you look at something you'd never noticed before, compelled into creative consideration you haven't quite grasped the gift of yet; face to face with something corresponding to your measure for wonder. Mountains hurdled, hearts opened, worries vanquished in the embrace of wheels, wind, and speed.

8

Defining What is Real

Childhood was rapidly flying past. Mom was in remission from the colon cancer she was diagnosed with when we were still small, Dad working at the same job he'd had since the '50s, soon to retire.

Our parents were older than all of our friends' parents, but we really didn't notice, not in a way that an adult would. Mom's auburn hair had gone gray, Dad's hair had flown south for the winter, and what little remained he kept in a military cut.

There was an advantage to having older parents. They certainly had more patience than some of our friend's parents—a necessary virtue when raising two redheads who were the very reason someone put "Cape does not enable user to fly" on a Halloween costume.

Allen and I never thought anymore about being adopted after that initial announcement. They were our parents, that's all we knew. I was curious as I approached my pre-teens, but I didn't want to ask my mom anything of my origins for fear that it would hurt her feelings. So I stayed silent.

At least we'd gotten past that brief time when Allen had me convinced that if I wasn't a perfect child they'd send us both back, resulting in much fear on my part and much less dirt tracked into the house. He was just joking; but like anything Allen told me, I believed him.

Such as the time he told me that the dog treat shaped like a chocolate candy kiss was really candy. At which point I popped it in my mouth. It wasn't awful, it just wasn't candy; but he couldn't wait to exclaim: "You're eating a dog treat; they're made out of cow pies and newspaper!" (Not true, that's the $1 frozen pizzas you can get at a big box mart). I went running to Mom in tears.

She looked up calmly and said: "Well, if you think you're going to get sympathy from me for believing everything your brother tells you, you're in for a surprise," and went back to her knitting.

Mom would defend us to the death from a grizzly bear or mountain lion; however, she refused to protect us from our own stupidity. She and Dad were our parents, and though we tried their patience and probably averted total mayhem just by luck more than once, they loved us.

So the thought of finding our biological parents just didn't occur to us at that age.

But always someone unthinking would ask: "So, have you tried to find your *real* parents?" Perhaps they meant well, but there's nothing more insulting to both adopted child and parent. We were with our *real* parents. We had no common genetics, but we shared a common experience, held tight within a web of love that knows not the blood but only a heart. Their creed was my only truth and their faithfulness to our care our only safety. These *were* my parents, in every way, shape, and fashion. And we were darn lucky to have them.

9

Looking Back

It's been well over forty years since Taylor's Mountain was dozed. I drove past the bustling subdivision that now stands in its place as I made another trip to see my family. Mom's been gone many years, the cancer finally claiming her. But Dad was happily remarried, as she had wished him to do, to a widow who treated Allen and me with love, still living in the house we grew up in.

It was nice to have a week of vacation with them, time to just sit must be cherished with all the constant travel; nothing to do but sit out on the porch and share stories. As we sat I watched a youngster go by on a bike, her mom walking behind her. The child had on a coat, gloves, a helmet, and knee pads. It was about 68 degrees. Put Allen and me on such a bike all those years ago and we'd have been bareheaded, barehanded, and probably in our shirtsleeves, Mom at home knowing we'd come back when we got hungry.

We were always in the company of other kids or a friend's older sibling, for even in small-town America a generation ago children could be prey. We rarely heard of such things before the Internet, but crimes against children occurred. My folks didn't push us into adulthood too soon, but they also taught us that the world is *not* necessarily a safe place, that with risk sometimes comes pain, and with danger there comes both exhilaration and consequence.

But I'd not trade that upbringing and the little scars that remain on me from it for anything. There's the one from a nasty cut on my foot playing cowboys and Indians barefoot on unfamiliar grounds. There is another where I got pelted with a piping hot stink bug from the Creepy Crawlers (we weren't protected from either the sun or heated toy appliances back in the day). There is a very faint line down my thumb from jousting with ink pens in honors math.

Good times.

It wasn't long before the freedom of those bicycles was replaced with the freedom of a car. My first one was an antiquated 1964 VW Bug, very cheap in so much that it was older than dirt and slower than molasses—but it was *mine*.

I remember those days as if it were yesterday; driving way too fast past streams that ran out of the higher elevations, veins that let the mountain bleed. The water rushed, tumbled, and raced to its destiny, to be drunk deeply or left to stagnate in a secluded pool. The sky would break out in articulate warmth there on those last days of the conceit of winter.

It was the end of the '70s. It was when I learned about freedom and speed, the year I learned to drive. It was the year in which I first learned about the hard outcome of choice.

I was always captured by movement, machinery, and speed; and now there were keys in my hand, a vehicle just waiting to take all of our compressed heat and explode it into sound. I started slowly, learning the basics, and then to drive in snow, gradually picking up speed. It wasn't long before my friends were driving with bigger, faster cars, and the speed would increase. We even found a road where, if you hit this rise just so and at a certain speed and angle, you could go airborne like *The Dukes of Hazard*.

We drove off into the hills with that sense of immortality that only the very young and the very stupid seem to have. Driving without fear, without thought, sacrificing only some rubber and the occasional fender to the gods of the roads. We were teens; there were tears and drama, hookups and breakups. It was the season of curving roads and youth; where we were immortal with no adult responsibilities to block that open road.

On those free afternoons we'd pile in the cars, heading up into the hills to seek the source of the water and ride it on down. Cresting the hills with windows open, the wind as fluid, hot, and hard as love, a swift current that will pull you under to drown, gasping. We'd drive for miles with just the sensation of rushing space as deep as the water. We'd drive until dark, unrelenting and unrepentant, curfews nipping at our heels, leaving in our wake only the sound of cicadas and the breathing of night taking in the remnant smell of high octane.

Soon enough there would be graduation and college, likely sans car to cut expenses. These days would vanish with a befitting and hollow sound, which would fall for only a moment upon us, with the dreadful hush of motion stopped too abruptly to mourn. Adulthood looming where vehicles became simply transportation again, something to shuffle kids around, a conveyance to work. We could not comprehend that someday, for many, life would become an emptying suitcase of enthusiasm. We swore if we ever had to buy a station wagon, we'd kill ourselves.

We had our future, we had our past; and in those moments, as wheels hit the pavement and gravel flew, sometimes we had both at once.

It was once said in an age-old axiom that an object cannot occupy two positions at the same time. Perhaps in those microscopic realms beyond any conceivable experiment of physics it will be possible somewhere, there in the darkened edges of our life where quantum mechanics reaches out to the human world. And we could be in two places at once. Or occupying the same position at two different times. Or fervently wishing we could.

I was working part-time at the local funeral home after school and on weekends; just someone in the building after hours in case a family came in, making coffee, doing light clerical work. My friends teased me, but they teased me as well when

I did career day with the forensic pathologists. The call came in late, a teen in a small car not unlike mine hit head on after they crossed the center line on a curve marked "no passing" to pass someone slower than their patience. There was probably only time enough for an intake of breath and hands flung up over his face, as if he could hide from that weighted shadow of choice which in that moment he had sacrificed himself for.

I was there when they brought him in. Though I didn't know him personally, I had more than one evening in his company there at the funeral home; and I wondered if he had second thoughts about his decision as he slept suspended within the hard vault of his regret.

Would he have made the same choices if he had known? We've all had days like that when simple things went awry—plans made that mattered little to you, but mattered much to others. Things said, bridges burned, moments that repeated themselves for weeks or months in your head. If only I'd done this, if only I'd said that. Moments in which you wish you could turn time back on itself, as if you'd never been there.

After that local tragedy our parents lectured us about the dangers of speed, about road signs and why they are there. Some kept their kids grounded, not allowing them to drive at all. Certainly such a place is safer; where no taint of desire affects debate and actions aren't directed by cloudy agendas. Still, it is a world flat and colorless as tap water. It's a world where, whether hiding at home or out with the wind in your face, we pass an anniversary without awareness. That of our own demise.

My Dad did not lecture, he knew what I'd seen was its own lesson. In a life fully lived we engage our fate deliberately; we speak the words we may later regret, but we have to say them. We engage life as an indefatigable opponent that others will wish to tiptoe by so as not to awaken it. We risk our necks and we risk our hearts. So although I slowed up it was not by much. But I didn't make it to adulthood by not scaring the wits out of myself, first in a car and later in an airplane as I took flying lessons; watching the earth go perpendicular and rush upwards as I hung on that last strand of lift above the deep yawn of gravity.

We've all been there—a carefully planned day meant to be spent in quiet order, when suddenly fate reaches out and places its hand on your shoulder; sometimes a reminder, sometimes an order home. The Earth is full of fight and friction; but when that moment happens the world hangs motionless in that instant, a cooling mass in space, even as you articulate your sudden surprise.

Sometimes you get lucky and survive, but the event leaves physical scars. But for most the scars can't be seen and can only be traced by inscrutable fingers, there in the dark while time ticks a reminder of battles sometimes lost.

I learned that as a teen as I dusted the coffins of those who had lost their particular battle. I learned later as I studied the bones and pieces of life past and present that fate is and always will be ravenous for the flesh of the foolish, rarely frustrated or even thwarted. It sits and waits with great patience, for yesterday and today are the same to it, indivisible, timeless. Sometimes it slumbers under God's stroking hand as he watches like a parent from a distance when we do something particularly foolish; sometimes it wakes up to solitary hunger that it will soon act upon.

Last night the phone rings late, but not as late as it sometimes does. My husband is sleeping and I quietly get ready to go. We're newlyweds, getting married twenty years after another marriage ended, and I give him a gentle kiss but not so as to wake him. I got called in to work. The work I do is not elemental to this story, one to tell perhaps when I retire, but it's a job of odd hours and often tragedy. It's what I believe I was always meant to do, I think as I grab my gear and warm up the big black truck sitting in the driveway. The cold echoes off the pavement in which the only shadow is its form. It's a large black truck, extended cab with a short bed.

As I climb in, I catch a reflection in the side window and see my own face. The face is of an adult yet overlaid with the plaintive need of the youth in all of us, seeking release, wanting to leave a parent's watchful eye and just feel the world soar past. I silently open the truck door as if sneaking out and fit my form into the leather seats, an old familiar embrace which no amount of days can change.

With a shuddering tremble of a racehorse at the gate, the truck backs out into the drive.

I have no curfew, just my wheels and miles of road interspersed with the angular cuts of barren fields, ringed with blue sky;

windows rolled up as a futile barrier to the outside elements. As the truck moves onward, rain begins to fall; an isolated thunderstorm. I watch the side of the road as ghosts of those who risked all wave at me from tiny markers that note their passing, and my foot comes off the gas, the water falling with astonishing clarity.

You need to look closely as you balance the deep satisfaction of taking a risk and winning with the need for caution; for weighing all the odds, the options, the infinity of what you are launching yourself into, is not easy. You take a risk of losing your life or losing your heart, both with consequences, both risks sometimes worth taking.

The water hits the hood and spreads, swimming like dew before a rush of air. One moment life and form, the next melting indistinguishably into the wind. Ahead are only the miles, with nothing to do but take in the occasional broken road sign and empty barns breaking up those small patches of cleared earth, whorled with hard work, small square islands of grain. The air is dense with the white smoke smell of brittle leaves, lying still like snow on the ground, fire in my heart. Up ahead the horizon, up above an inscrutable sky, desolate above the land over which it looms. On the seat is a heavy flashlight, there if I need it, one less shadow to flee through and from.

I'm wondering if this rig will go airborne if I hit the rise just so—but I don't, knowing when it's time to speed past that demarcation between what I should do and what my heart tells me to do. Calculating the miles, the speed, the wind, the traffic;

weighing the risks of life versus loss. The passing landscape is bounty and beholder, the open road its postulate. The asphalt flows past, as do the signs—of feed stores, of gas stations, of tiny fixed crosses there by the road. Reminders that despite our freedoms there are lines that are written into infinity. Once you cross them you can never go back.

10

Snow Days

It seemed like those childhood years were a blink. Our dog Pepper had crossed the Rainbow Bridge; Dad was getting ready to retire. Before I knew it Allen was off to the Navy, going to submarine school, myself already in college, working toward my commercial pilot's license. I ultimately wanted a career in science or criminal justice, perhaps both—but as a teen I got a second job at the local airport pumping gas. I could get flying lessons at a reduced cost, so I was working toward my license while cramming in way more classes than I had hours in the day. For that kind of overextending, there is a "complete breakfast"—which for me was Hostess Sno Balls and coffee, grabbed when a parent wasn't looking. Unhealthy yes, but just the taste of them took me back. It was that and the big bowl of Captain Crunch before every flight check. I was glad years later when I got my nickname as a pilot that it was "Shake and Bake" and *not* "Captain Crunch."

Still—all good memories. Memories of childhood are so different for many people. I am lucky that mine were good. Laughter and exploration wrapped in a warm blanket of sight and sound and tastes that are still on my tongue. Memories of the past are like that; often having an impossible quality of perfection we frequently give to material things, a favorite book, a favorite tool or firearm; sometimes to a whole relationship we can never get back to.

If we could only get there again, have that again, hold that again, our lives would somehow be better; as if some cold case crime was finally solved, the reminders of things that hurt us left behind, held in our mind never to be freed again.

We've all talked about it, some small trivial thing from the past that appears to contain the sublime, and there's no explaining it to anyone, try though you might. Still, in your mind's eye it's there and always will be as clear and as sure as if it were yesterday. For me one such memory is opening up the lunch box as a kid and finding my Hostess treat next to my peanut butter and honey sandwich, apple, and carrot sticks.

Mom's cancer was one of those things that will stay with me for a lifetime. She was first diagnosed in the early '60s. The long term survival rate for her type of cancer then was only one in seven. When she was first diagnosed, she was only in her forties. I was not even in school yet, Allen only a couple of years older. She came home after Christmas that first time, chemo shunt in place, and did everything in her power to make our life normal.

I don't recall her initially leaving for the hospital, only the worried look in my dad's eyes. But the photos bring it back, like the one of my brother at her hospital bed with a little aluminum tree on the nightstand—as she holds up a flannel nightgown Dad picked out and bought "from us" that she opened from her hospital bed.

The doctor's treatment did not cure her, but it gave her quite a few more Christmas mornings, including the one where Allen and I pooled our allowances and bought her a nightgown *we picked out all by ourselves*. It was red, see-through, and very short, trimmed with fake fur that was shedding like a polecat with mange even as we wrapped the gift ourselves. I'm not sure *what* discount place on Main Street we got it from, but young as we were we thought it was quite spiffy, and oh, won't our quiet, cookie-baking mom love this! I still remember the fits of laughter she tried to suppress when she opened the package and held up the nightgown. (Dad seemed to like it, though.)

I remember her making our school lunches with homemade cookies if she was up to it, and our Hostess treats when she wasn't. It was Ding Dongs for Allen, Sno Balls for me. I'd eat one at lunch and take the remaining one to the playground after school, eating it perched on top of the biggest, tallest pieces of playground equipment I could find; defying gravity, feet dangling in the air, Mom watching carefully from a distance. Then we'd go home to start supper, eager to tell both Dad and Mom about our day, and we'd listen to her laugh—that sound, the stored honey of her spirit, carried on wings whose load was heavy, delivered to us, her children, to make us whole.

I remember the snow days when school was canceled. Mom

would hand us our snow gear and off we'd go. Another day of adventure. We'd grab our inner tubes and go barreling down the snow-laden slopes of the neighborhood park, with no admonishments to "Be careful!" or "Did you brush your teeth?" or "You're tracking snow into the house!" On such days we were just allowed to be kids and for just that unique time to be completely carefree. When we were so cold and tired we could barely stand with scrapes and giggles and bruises, we'd tromp back to the house for hot chocolate and a sweet baked treat.

Before cancer, our list of should-dos was really quite long. And like other families that cope with disappointment or disease we quit using the work "should" quite so much. The house may have been be a bit messier; but given the choice of cleaning or building a snowman with her kids, doing that ironing now or joining us in a snowball fight, her choice went toward those small joys.

Still, Mom maintained her discipline as a mother; and for every sweet snack we got there were still those family dinners where you had better eat your vegetables. She and I had a doctrine of mutually assured destruction involving acorn squash. She refused to not make it, and I refused to eat it—sitting at the table long after everyone else was excused, the squash growing as chilly as that Veggie Cold War; until finally she gave up and sent me to my room without dessert, something that was not easy on either of us.

I was too young to appreciate the depth of what she did for us, instilling in us love for each other and appreciation for the blessings of our table. But I was old enough to see that courage is simply the power to see past misfortune or expectation, to hold on to the things that affirm inwardly that life with all its trials is still good. Be it a warm hug or sweet treats handed to us with a smile and a touch on our head, a benediction of love that could only come from the wellspring of faith that stayed within her.

I cannot, no matter how hard I try, remember her voice; but if I close my eyes I can remember that touch. It was not a touch as heavy and uncaring as a slap, but one that simply said: I love you, but you must have courage and craft your life for yourself, just let me share it as long as I can.

Watching us spread our wings, knowing she would likely be gone before we were grown with families of our own, had to have been so hard. Like any mother she was concerned with our safety, but never to the point where we were wrapped in bubble wrap, spoiled, and coddled, or given everything we wanted without effort. We worked hard for our allowance, doing chores; but when the chores were done, we were encouraged to go explore the world around us.

Myself, I'd get on my bike and go ride the dusty gash of a roadway near the railroad tracks, where I could see and hear the trains go by—the engine passing in hissing thunder, sparks flying up like fireflies let loose from the rails, dust coiling behind it like a tornado in trail. Such began my adventures, my love of motion and machinery.

We had no timetable, yet we always seemed to know when the train would come by. One moment the tracks would be empty, the next filled with the rhythmic rumble of sound, of life that materialized seemingly out of nothing; with an air of the deliberately accidental that lingered like smoke long after it disappeared from sight. I stopped my bike and simply stood watching, compelled to pause—still in that infinite clutch of the temporary confederation of two elements, water and air; the frailest of integers and units of measure combing into a force that cannot be bound, not even in death.

Such is memory, such is life. Those moments that perhaps were predestined, glimpsed only so briefly before they are gone; those memories that come with smell or sound that linger. Memories plucked from the infinitesimal, with infinitesimal longing.

We crammed a lot of life into those short childhood years, as did our mom. More than we expected her to have, but not nearly enough. It's been a lifetime since she left us, and all that remains are the memories—memories that come on the wings of a snowfall; that raise a smile every time I see an acorn squash at the grocery store; that rumble into life with the roar of a locomotive or the soft crackle of a little cellophane package being gleefully opened by eager hands.

It was five in the morning. In a few hours I would have to get up and go to the airport to fuel the aircraft for the morning students, cram in some studying, and then ride my bike to the community college for class. The alarm went off much too early, my hand slapping it even as it gently touched a photo of

Allen and me as children, Pepper the wiener dog lying between us as we watched *Johnny Quest*.

Outside, the moonlight filters through darkened trees, their branches raised up as if in prayer. From a distance comes the whistle of a train, the mournful sound carried on the windless cold that is memory's heat. Inside, the rest of the house sound asleep, there is only quiet and another photo on my desk, of a tall young woman with dark auburn hair and ice-blue eyes in a simple wooden frame.

I know there is oatmeal and fruit in the kitchen; but in the cupboard I found one last package of Sno Balls. I think this one time Mom would not mind if I had one for breakfast. I'll put on my coat and head out on the porch; perhaps eating the Sno Ball as I perch on the wooden railing, feet dangling into the air just for one more moment—ignoring the inherited perpetual recognition of gravity, while Mom watches over me even as heaven sleeps.

11

Leaving the Nest

One of the rites of passage into adulthood in my generation, outside of the coveted driver's license, was getting your first apartment. It seems most of us couldn't wait to have our own place, even if it was bereft of any furniture not normally seen on the patio, or any other creature comfort.

For some it might be during or after college, for some it might be after college or the military, but there is no getting past the memory: that first taste of independence was like your first significant kiss. It seems like years ago though it's not, yet you can still remember the taste, how you felt; like a match burning without a source of ignition, waiting for something to set alight.

When Allen was finally stationed at a submarine base on the same coast as me, I flew a small Piper airplane to see him after getting directions to his base housing. I was still working on building the required hours for my single engine airplane commercial rating. I missed him, feeling like only half of myself when he wasn't around.

Allen's place was easy to pick out among the identical battle-ship-gray dwellings, a tale I've told many times, his being the only one with the *For Sale by Owner* sign and a herd of pink plastic flamingos around it.

That wasn't his first place though. I remember Allen's first apartment post high school graduation while he was working at Montgomery Ward Auto Center. It was a two bedroom place that he shared with a couple of buddies. The carpet was this horrid shag that was less "clean and fresh" and more the chip and hamburger crumbles equivalent of a body farm. Their de-cor consisted of a couple of chairs and a display made of what appeared to be every imported beer they'd drunk since gradu-ation, the bottles carefully dried and set up against the wall in some sort of artistic display of German expressionism.

Being the solitary type, my first place was a tiny apartment on the fifth floor in an old brick building. There were no elevators, but it was in a clean, safe neighborhood with lots of parking. Too bad I could no longer afford a car. But it was near the bus line, I had a bike, and my best friend had a car if I got stuck.

My furniture consisted of a beanbag chair, a couple of lawn chairs, and a bed. I'd have friends over, and the older ones would bring wine. But these weren't the alcohol-fueled parties of my peers or even my brother's buddies. We'd bring books and we'd discuss history and science, both fiction and non-fiction. I'd make coffee for the younger crowd, and we'd ban-ter about Calvin and Hobbes long before they were a cartoon. Those were good evenings, as we gently sipped on a drink in a serious, almost celibate way as the conversations went late into the night. There was nothing better.

Until I got homesick.

The first couple of months were grand, staying up as late as I wanted (well, late, given I was going to school and working thirty hours a week), leaving my books lying all over the place without the family dog using them as chew toys. I could have pizza for breakfast, Bologna sandwiches for lunch, and more pizza for dinner (if an apple is in the room, that counts as your serving of fruit for the day). I could play the radio as loud as my neighbors would allow, which was generally louder than what parents would permit—if you're living in a building that's mostly full of young people, at least on the fifth floor.

But when you trudge up five flights of stairs to come home, there's no one there with a snack who says, "So, what have you been up to?" As kids, that was the best part of the day, coming home to a mom who gave up a great career just to be there to make sure we were fed, loved, and educated. We used to rush in from play like stampeding cattle, poured a glass of milk, and sat down to cookies or whatever she made (which during her cancer treatment was often just frosting between graham crackers, all she had the strength for, though she'd brightly tint the frosting just for us).

We'd chatter away until the sugar buzz wore off, get a big hug, and go tend to our chores.

As I walked into that first apartment, greeted only by mute dust bunnies, I realized I missed all that. I missed dinner as a family around the table, the saying of grace as we held hands. I even missed Dad admonishing me as I trailed in dirt when I brought in a fresh load of firewood, yet always making sure I was safely in my bed at night; a quiet closing of my door against the noise in the living room, his feet a thick whisper in the hallway as my eyes closed in safety and peace.

I missed my mom.

But there was so much to do now that I didn't have a lot of time for reminiscing. Not only did I have a full load of college classes, there was still my job at the airport pumping gas when I wasn't in school. The weather seemed to be one of two choices: desert hot or a dark chill that pelted my skin and hands with sleet like little daggers of ice, the wind so strong that the flame from a departing F-4 fighter jet shed away like fiery streamers as I stood and watched and yearned.

Then there was the other job at the local funeral home chain where I worked weekends, which I had through high school. That job was ideal for a student. It was their rural location, without a funeral director on nights and weekends unless called, and it paid more than minimum wage.

I had few responsibilities unless a body was brought in or a family stopped by due to a sudden death. In both cases I knew what to do, and aside from some light housekeeping and an occasional invoice to process, the rest of the twelve-hour shift was mine to do schoolwork. I learned how to dress and act like a grown-up. I learned how to make really good coffee. I learned how to say "I'm sorry for your loss," and truly feel it. I learned what "closed casket" often really means.

For both Allen and me, having our own place without "Mom!" was an eye-opener. Laundry, I discovered, did not magically do itself; and as many times as I stood in front of the refrigerator, it never spit out a meal like a food replicator on a galaxy class starship.

And between rent, food, bus fare, tuition, and books, there was no money for much else. I applied for student loans but was always turned down with "your family income is too high." I tried to explain my dad was not paying for my college, *I was.* We were raised where you either put yourself through college, as Mom and Dad did, or you joined the military. Once you were eighteen, you were on your own financially.

It sounds harsh, but my parents grew up in the first Great Depression, my mom the offspring of generations of Scandinavian seafarers. My great uncle was a captain of his own ship, the *Marie Bakke*; other relatives less well known yet not forgotten, even if quietly tapping their bones together at the bottom of a cold sea.

Dad grew up dirt-poor, getting through college with ROTC and a full-time job on campus.

But like our parents and grandparents before us, we were

expected to make our own way; and the last time I was turned down for a student loan, I looked at the lady who said I didn't qualify and said, "Have you ever eaten an oatmeal sandwich?"

Being a young adult had its perks, but a high standard of living wasn't one of them. But I learned a lot during that time. How to fix what little I owned (duct tape *was* a repair); how a slow cooker from the Salvation Army could make meals for the freezer for a week for less than the cost of some blue boxes of pasta; how filling bra cups up with cotton and wrapping them around your head does *not* make a good set of ear protection when the neighbor on the other side of the thin wall has an all-night date with that was either an overly sexed blonde or a wolverine (hard to tell with the noise).

It taught me about working so hard that when the shift was over I'd lie down on a hard floor in a back room and sleep, unable to stand on my feet long enough to get to a bunk. It taught me about the riotous joy in the smallest of things: the taste of rich soup, the sweet wine of both freedom and communion, the tender kiss of support from the ones that see you through all of the battles.

A lifetime later my brother and I would still both lie on opposite sides of the country, in simple beds in simple houses. Mine was a hundred years old, Allen's not much newer. He had no home computer; I had a phone the size of a boat anchor whose only app was the "ringing" one. None of our dishes matched, and there were more books than any other single type of item in either of our homes. As we both lay quietly before sleep, we listened to the wind, to the sound of the wood of the houses around us, a wood that neither bends nor moans. The wood itself was still, as are bones that quiet when the reflexes of earthly compulsions have expended themselves.

Hard times and lean times are only forever if you believe they are. If you refuse to, they are simply brief glances in which, for a moment without measure or context, will lie in your sights the portent of all that you think you cannot bear but will, there between the darkness and the light.

12

Clear Cut

Clear cut—clear and certain, so that there is no doubt about something.

Looking back on these stories of growing up, I see that few things in life are clear or certain.

In a small dish on my desk in my office is a rough gemstone. My mom and I both collected gemstones, so they are something I've been receiving as gifts ever since childhood, some beautiful beyond measure. This one on my desk is plain, but it has a history. Its edges are sharp, defined, its color muted. Given to me when I was still so young and vulnerable by someone who once laid the cold stone in my hand, as a memento of a fine day—while his eyes looked off into the distance to a place that would not include me. There was a good age difference between us. I was headstrong and fiery and in love for the first time; and he said he tired of doing battle with women, with a lot of things. Still a teenager, I was too young to know that even if he had chosen to stay, the relationship would turn as sharp and as brittle as glass; but it didn't make the end any easier on me. I'd lost my innocence that summer, never to be regained.

I still keep the stone, and I occasionally pick it up and hold it—the mass in my hand real, tangible, carrying with it the weight of astonishing clarity.

I think with a brain that is both artist and scientist, the logical part of me making decisions based on a summary of tangents, rules, lines, and engineering. Yet my heart tends to run on up ahead into the traffic, shouting into the wind. I put the stone down where it lay on some dried yellow flowers, a reminder of clear thinking, hard choices, tears that can carve the hardest stone.

Clear cut—clear and certain.

That summer I was well into my college program, starting to go to classes at the community college part-time at age fourteen; something that came about after the school called the house to tell my parents I was skipping school, and did they know where I was? Dad said, "Sure—she's at the library." You can imagine the teacher's reaction—"She's skipping school to go to the *library*?" Dad explained to her that I wasn't challenged. This was a factory town where ninety percent of the kids who graduated would take a well-paying job there or in a supporting business and never leave. Next thing I knew, I was taking some of my standard high school classes at the local college and going full-time in the summer.

I was still pumping gas at the local airport in exchange for money and lessons. My love of motion and speed extending well beyond cars—though my career aspirations were science, not aviation—I soon had my pilot's license, a commercial one for small aircraft. I got a job flying aerial fire patrol during the summer to accumulate flight hours, saving money so I could transfer to a large university in "the big city" if I chose not to go into the military like my brother did.

I liked that type of flying. There was no rush; I kept the horizon in my window but still looked down, savoring the journey, taking meticulous mental notes of what I was seeing to pass on, looking for any sign of smoke here in what they called "hoot owl" days. It was a great way to earn some money, watching tumbled landscapes of glacier stone and great pristine rivers as thin as a strand of pearls from up here. The day proceeded in the immaculate sameness of hours bathed in the sun's warm honey. Thoughts flowed, only interrupted by a needed scan as I noted the large stretches of mountain completely barren of trees and other areas where replanting had begun.

Clear cut.

It was fall, the fire season almost past, those polished days of heat. The long awaited cool mornings that gave themselves up to surreal afternoons, the land surrendering its thirst to the amber ale of autumn.

In what now seems a lifetime ago, there was the loss of a fire crew, one that has probably been forgotten to most. A large tanker plane returning after a long day of fire suppression, on its way back to base to a well-earned night of relaxation. It was my first summer working as an aerial fire patrol pilot—perfect summer employment for a college student; and I'd met and made friends with a number of pilots on various bases who did such flying. I never thought about the risks. As a teenager I was too enthralled with the aerial adventure to even think about the dangers of what we did each day. That night I was even less concerned, as I was tired and not feeling well. I'd been feeling out of sorts for the last few weeks, weary and sick to my stomach, so I declined an invitation to go out with school friends and settled in for a book and a nap.

A dear friend was on board the flight that night, a mentor and fellow pilot. That night he was just catching a ride in the back and called to say goodbye to me after he'd gotten off the phone with his girlfriend. He wasn't my boyfriend—not the dashing fellow who had given me the stone. John was just my pal, my confidant, and someone I could talk about flying with. I'd met his girlfriend, another potential new friend, scarce to be found when there are few hours in the day to be social with anyone other than classmates.

We'd just gone out for a burger the previous week to celebrate John's upcoming interview with a major airline, the goal for which he'd survived several summers of sweat, dirt, and danger; a goal others in his small town said he'd never obtain. "I'll call you in a few days, after the interview. . . . Fly safe, kiddo," he said and hung up. Soon they were airborne, while the visages of smoke from the day's fires clung to the ridges like a sigh.

I hung up the phone and opened the book I was reading; and an hour later John was dead, the plane down in a fiery ball. Afterward I tried to find something to explain what had happened—was there a mechanical failure? Was there a thunderstorm hidden in smoke and encroaching dark? But the night was ordinary. I think it usually is when your life implodes. Most people aren't doing anything special when tragedy reaches out and catches them by the sleeve. An investigation was launched, probable cause debated. I didn't care about that. All I cared about was that my friend was gone—John, only twenty-six years old.

The funerals were crowded with pilots and firefighting personnel. Solemnly laying them to rest, we then took to the skies with a small salute of loss . . . That is, all of the pilots but me: an hour after John's funeral I had received a call from my doctor, because I'd finally scheduled an exam to find out why I was feeling so bloated and tired the last couple of months.

I was pregnant.

When the words passed from the doctor's assistant to my brain, cold air slipped down my body and the room grew close. I thought I was so tough, so experienced for my age; and there I was, a scared, unwed nineteen-year-old with a cupboard full of Ramen noodles and $75 to my name. I sat and cried, passively and plaintively, like a small child in the dentist's waiting room.

Of that moment I remember little else. Was it raining? Was the sun out? I don't remember, but the day was ordinary. It usually

is when your life changes. Most people aren't really doing anything noteworthy when the carefully guarded and fragile pieces
of their lives shatter with something they never expect.

You never know when something is going to happen to change
your life. You think fate will arrive with fanfare, but instead
it comes in the most ordinary of circumstances. You expect a
large brown bear, but it's naught but a spider dangling from a
beam, twisting and turning in the wind, striking you with the
smallest of touch that can bring either wonder or intense fear.
Most people are usually not prepared for either.

All I knew was that I had to make a choice about what to do
with my life, this baby. We make choices from such limited information. From the sweet words of lovers, to slogans, to cam-
paign promises. How do you know how to make the right one?

After the crash, with this sudden change in my life and no
friends to counsel me, I made my decision, with only my heart
and the values of my parents to guide me. I had been adopted,
my brother had been adopted. Yes, I was old enough to quit
school and get a job and raise my baby, but I wanted her to
have more. I wanted my child to have the life that I had been
given, even if I had parents who never relented on the whole
"flamethrower" request.

After I told my Dad, and he simply hugged me, I sat in a fuzzy
yellow bathrobe in my old room, on a little bed under child-
ish rainbows painted on the walls. I sat motionless, breathing
deep and steady until the sun began to set. It wasn't so much

the sun setting but rather that the light simply condensed into a smaller space, much like a damaged heart.

The wind gasped against curtains, a soft whoosh that I realized was my own breathing. My heart, my breath, my blood, all entwined with new life now in this quiet space. Even if I held my breath, his or her little heart would keep on beating.

So I did not make the choice that many would, the easy way out. I considered every option, but I knew what I could live with, and that was to have her. But as a full-time student I knew I'd not be able to raise her; the baby's father, having been married and divorced, did not want any part of us in his future, which he was brutally clear about as he shoved me out of his life.

No, there was only one choice for me: to provide this life within me with the best future possible. Rather than worry about the past and what I could not change, I learned to fight as the future progressed, knowing that most anything was possible if I put my mind to it. That was my friend John's legacy to me: live strong, own up to your mistakes, and work hard for your freedoms—for the end can come in a blink of the sun in your eyes, in a flash of fire.

The doctor said the baby would be born sometime before the new year. I moved back home, not having the money for doctors and an apartment; appreciating that my family didn't attempt to keep it a secret. Dad certainly didn't approve of my actions that resulted in this pregnancy, but he was never ashamed of me. We got through the next few months as best as we could, awaiting that birth.

We all have chased the wind and danced with the flames, sometimes getting singed, sometimes being honed in the fire. Fighting fire is dangerous work, and those that have done it wonder if the gains of it ever balance the costs. Yet for those of us who have walked that path, we will always acknowledge that among the ruins something bright and lasting can be found.

I pick up the crystal again from its little spot among the dried yellow flowers. The sun catches it, and it burns with amethyst fire, clear and with purpose.

13

Outcomes

I looked at myself closely in the mirror, wondering just how this pregnancy had happened. Oh, I knew the "how"—I was in the middle of a degree program that was veering back and forth between engineering, criminal justice, and the forensic sciences.

I was not the face of teen pregnancy. I was from a sound, middle-class Christian home with loving parents who had adopted me as an infant and provided time, morals, and balance in my early formative years. My mom left a career in law enforcement to be a full-time mother and did so with the values of generations. I was the girl who still wore dresses to school long after everyone only wore jeans, and I didn't mind. I was a straight-A student, a volunteer, and a National Honor Society member.

And I had fallen in love—with the breathtaking tumble that you think you'll only experience once in your life and grab onto like a lifeline. We'd met in a summer college course I had taken in addition to my high school classes. We talked as if we'd always be together. He introduced me to his two young daughters from an earlier marriage. I didn't tell my family of my feelings. Did it mean that they were not there to listen? Did it mean they were too busy? No, I was a teenager; and at that age you don't tell your family members everything, nor do you make the best decisions even with the best of parenting. And one night, just one time, I listened to him and not my upbringing. I made the wrong choice.

When I told my love I was pregnant, I expected he would marry me or at least offer. I was still a teen but he was older, with a job and a home; and legally I was an adult. He did not offer to marry me. He very cruelly and coldly offered me enough money to "take care of the problem," and then he left me. I thought I was part of his dreams and plans—but suddenly I was alone; and all that remained was the huge question of where this new destination in my life would take me.

He meant nothing of what he had told me; he had no interest in marriage, in family; words only spoken to get me into bed, just another conquest.

I had no one to blame but myself.

But teen pregnancy was very different in those days. Back then no one showed up with reality TV cameras and wads of cash, making someone a television star just for being dumb enough to believe some guy's line. If they had made a show out of this, it wouldn't have been called *Teenage Mom*, but more like: *Was I an Idiot or WHAT?*

No, I just had to deal with it. I might have been advanced academically, but in essence I was only a teenager. I was scared and angry at myself as I first prayed, "Oh please don't let me be." I had not known with certainty that life itself grew in each single, shining moment, even the ones you regret. I had not grasped the wonder that can be found in a simple forming of cells, the flutter of life from the womb when I lay sleeping, hand protectively across my belly. I had not yet witnessed an acceptance that cleanses one of fear and anger. As I sat at the piano, quietly tapping out a single note, I did not fully understand how music can be both joy and sadness, both of them consecrated.

I didn't know any of this yet. I only knew that we were all destined to die—some before our time.

But in this case I would do what I could for this one small soul—to make sure it had a chance to live, though I had no clue what I would do with my life afterward. I only knew at this time that I would bear in silence, and perhaps pain, a new life into the world.

Beyond that—the music was silent.

14

Book of Names

I look back on a faded old photo—my standing by a small aircraft, my pregnancy finally starting to show. My head was up, hair cut short as I was still working and going to school. With a pregnancy on top of it there was not much time for beauty, and my heart was in no place to wish to find anyone to appreciate it.

I look around me now at this house I share with my new husband, a lifetime after that scared young girl sat and wondered about her fate; two decades after a scared young woman left a young marriage of anger and heartache with only the clothes on her back and a picture of a baby on the dashboard.

Such journeys we take, I think as I trace my new last name on my driver's license.

I was surprised how much was involved with changing my last name. One doesn't realize how many different places it is listed, not just Social Security and driver's licenses, but credit cards, e-mail, and shopping haunts. Then there are my airmen certificates and my passport. Not to mention a gazillion different computer passwords. But not changing it when I married never occurred to me; I'm old-fashioned that way, wishing to honor the name of my husband as he honors me. Out of habit I still I occasionally sign a document with my former name, my administrative assistant just grinning and getting me a new one to sign.

I had the old name a long time, wearing it as hammers were swung and nails were bent. I donned it in white and wore it through blood—until one day that swung hammer built a door I could walk through and never look back. It just seemed easier to keep it, that name I wore like a bruising for twenty years on my own. People knew me by that name professionally. But this new name, this name is mine forever, even after it is written in stone.

The sciences were my subjects in school, and walking through an excavation, through a field, I can name things: trees, plants, animals. *Acer diabolicum*, *Canis latrans*, *Mephitis mephitis* (run, guys, run!), *Chrysomya rufifacies*. Latin (quite often a mixture of Latin and Greek) was the language used by educated people and by the church in older times, so Latin was used to give scientific names to animals and plants. The names weren't just given randomly, though. They meant something.

The knights of the Middle Ages were known by just one name. They rode with the name that was worn with chivalry, honor displayed with honor, courage proclaimed with courage. Bravery was more about the deed than the actual doing;

something deemed worthy even if in doing so they merely proved that death does not retreat and some battles were best left unfought. Just a name can take us back to furious history, where sometimes all that is left of the battle is jagged metal twisted into living ground, annealing into that which it drove into head-on. That is often a path as swift and narrow as glory itself, until glory is gone and all that remains is the weeping earth.

I recently read a book about the Lewis and Clark expedition. Lewis and Clark did more than chart, they named. Apparently, they named everything they ran across that didn't already have a name: spots of land, and trees like the lodge pole pine, *Pinus contorta*, trees twisted and stunted by Pacific coast storms. They named birds, the Lewis's woodpecker and the Clark's nutcracker. They named the waters they traveled down. They named the places in which they camped.

Simple acts, simple words for things that have a deep and different significance for everyone that hears them. What did Lewis and Clark think when they saw the mighty Pacific Ocean for the first time, standing in awe as a roaring wave broke with fury at their feet? As the waters receded they gave it a name, a word that broke in an instant with a sound that would remain as long as people were alive to hear it. In some religions it is believed that people cannot be granted eternal life until they have been baptized, until they have been given a name.

Yet we do not know God's name. In all the world's religions that I have read of, there is no revelation or rationalization of

God as clear and powerful to me as the name that he spoke to Moses. "I AM WHO I AM." The power to name is the power to create, and the power to create is the power to destroy.

People have birth names and nicknames. I have the name that was on my adoption papers. I have the name I use in work. I have a title. "Doc" is not a nickname but it's a title I only use when I have to, for in certain venues of the law it wields some power. I have the name that only my brother could get away calling me. They are all part of me, in all their forms they describe me. As little girls we give our dolls names to bring them to life. My favorite childhood doll is still in my room at home, where I see her from my bed at night when I'm visiting, sitting quietly below twisting stars—an oblivious playmate, now silenced by adulthood.

I remember the night my daughter was born after thirty-four hours in labor, her head crowning, her body bursting forth onto the sweat- and blood-soaked sheet. I remember only getting to hold her once, for just a moment before I handed her over to her adoptive parents; incredulous of her soft hair, perfect fingers, smelling of the womb, of warmth, of love. She looked at me with a peripheral glance, while I uttered the name I would give her and the words I was not able to say again for years, for in fear of their utterance the object of my words would be lost to me. *I love you.*

As adults we name our pets to make them members of the family. God called life from the fluid chaos of creation by calling its name. We call home our own loved ones with a name, yelled across the back porch into seeping twilight. Time to come in, time to come home. We outlive them, then raise our toasts to them, the red hot Pentecostal peat that echoes from a shot glass, a wafer taste of smoke against the tongue, drops of amber liquid on the table like tears.

There are some living things that define classification, and thus defy being named. *Protists*—groups of living things comprising those living things which are neither animal, plant, nor fungi. Protists—the scientist's way of saying "none of the above." One of them is algae. Bones are affected under the earth by algae, fungi, and bacteria. Under a microscope the traces of damage due to fungi or algae appear as horizontal or vertical channels. These channels sometimes converge on one another to form large flat or tufted forms, causing the entire bone to disintegrate—in some rare cases destroying all one might have left to identify someone by name.

Sometimes all that is left to be buried are a few teeth, a piece of bone. But it is at least something to be placed in the ground with a name. Something for remembrance, for closure. On my long drive into the city I see the occasional cross by the road, with simply a name and perhaps a few flowers. How important these undistinguished little memorials. Every death is a memory that ends here, yet continues on. Enduring, for there is not one of us who can affirm that there must be a web of muscle and bone to hold the conformation of love. It's there in dust and sky and new life. It's there in the shadow of a half moon, quivering in the sky like a heel print in wet sand, a large piece of rock that man has named but few would walk. It's there within us, in that place that resists narrative, deep within, waiting.

So what is in a name? It is memory; something that is not simply particular, it is also tutelary, foretelling. In the end it is as reliable as we are, as strong as our word. The names and facts of my life by themselves are insignificant. But what our names represent is history, a life. When I look at the name of someone I loved on a gravestone I do not see stone, I do not see letters. I see remembrance, and that is what we keep on living for. A simple name brings back memories, like a plunge underwater in a swift stream; an airplane baffled and bounced in a fierce wind; a stillness and persistence of going forward alone.

I trace the outline of a name, and I know how that name made me feel. And that is not insignificant. I hear my name across hundreds of electronic miles of science, breathed into a phone late at night, and I know the warm rush of healing that comes with that one word.

For earth without form is void, but heaven without names is only blackness.

15

Love's Labor

I was going to name the baby Justin if it was a boy, or Grace after my mother if it was a girl. Grace. I knew her new parents would likely change it, but that was the name I would carry on my heart until I saw my child again.

I'd made the decision to give the baby up for adoption, giving him or her the same chance at a loving family, the safety net of structure and financial security that Allen and I had known growing up. I also wanted the child to have two parents and perhaps other siblings someday.

But I wanted to know who my child would be placed with, so I would not have to wonder if he or she was in the best environment. Things worked out, as they have a way of doing. My doctor knew a couple who had been successfully vetted to adopt and had been on the waiting list for a long time, relatives of a local nurse. They were kind, hardworking people, desperately longing for a child; with a stable home and a modest but sufficient means to raise her. I trusted this doctor and agreed to talk to the adoption agency to see if this family would be a good match for my child. I never met them in person, I just signed papers—as did the baby's biological father, thankfully when I was not present. It was not to be a truly open adoption where I would be able to see the child as she grew up; but her prospective parents had stated they would support her meeting me as an adult if that was what she wished.

And so it was done, fall giving way to winter, my belly growing more enormous, my wondering if I'd ever be happy again—wondering if I'd ever see my *toes* again. Flying in a little Spam can of an airplane was out of the question, and the fumes of fueling weren't good to be around while pregnant, so I got another job typing for a local business, along with two other rotating part time jobs.

Christmas came and went. The doctor thought I was on schedule—I *knew* I was past my due date. He and I differed in our opinions on that, but unlike him I was there when the pregnancy happened and remembered the date. After some bit of ticklish torture in the hospital's radiology department, which involved drinking about a quart of water and then having jelly rubbed on my skin so the image technicians could get a good look at the baby, it was determined I was truly at full term. It was time to help things along as I was *not* going to go into labor on my own and this child was not willing to come out.

At this point I realized the baby was going to be a female and red-haired. Call it mother's instinct.

I'd watched childbirth on TV. There was some sweat and some grunting, and then the baby would come into view—squeaky clean, wrapped in a blanket. In the very next shot the mother was miraculously wearing mascara and lip gloss, none the worse for wear but for a single bead of sweat upon her brow.

My brother had married a woman with a young daughter whom he adopted. I remember my sister-in-law telling me she was only in labor about an hour and a half and had had the baby forty-five minutes after arriving at the hospital. I figured this wouldn't be that hard.

Twenty hours into labor I had changed my mind. I was glad they kept the sharp objects and the alcohol hidden away; and I also noted how much quicker other women were coming in and out of the maternity ward—except for that one woman whose husband said, "Can you be quiet honey, I'm trying to watch the game," only to be forcefully tossed from the room by someone half his size.

The labor had to be induced. Apparently I didn't produce the hormone that caused one to go into labor; and it took a couple of days with a Pitocin drip to start the action. Once it began it was like watching golf. Actually it was like watching golf while being waterboarded. But because I'd been induced, they didn't want to do anything to slow down an already slow labor, so serious pain medication until she was on the way out was only a distant dream. This was going to be a natural childbirth whether I liked it or not.

She was born. I had prayed that it would not happen. Now someone new and perfect lay sleeping sweet dreams of her whole life ahead as two good people who had pretty much given up had their own dreams fulfilled. When the news came that she was born and was ready for them, her new parents were in Hawaii, where her mother was from. Her dad walked outside in the warm night air and promptly threw up, perhaps believing that I would change my mind, perhaps just overwhelmed by the thought of it all. For it likely hit them all at once: they were going to be parents—and right now.

Grace, with hope. Hope—something I did not know I had been lacking until that moment. That moment I prayed would be only a false alarm instead now becoming my biggest act of faith: her name a remembrance to the one who saved me so long ago.

I called my love, not expecting anything. He had already signed the consent for adoption papers; I just wanted to let him know he had a daughter, his third, as he had two with his ex-wife. He told me he was getting married to his business partner and to never call again. At point, tears on my face, one of the nurses came in to see me. I was not sure what to say to her, and she sat down and softly started humming a little song:

> *If you go down to the woods today*
> *You're sure of a big surprise,*
> *If you go down to the woods today*
> *You're better go in disguise,*
> *For every bear that ever was there*
> *Will gather there for certain because*
> *Today's the day the Teddy Bears*
> *Have their picnic.*

I smile and hum along, the nurse's hands clasping mine. Then she leaves, with my life. I am determined to be strong, to smile, to not say goodbye. Never goodbye. The big beige door swing shuts behind them. Then quiet. Dad comes in and tries to talk to me of hope. He talks of being brave and the past and a future, and he urges me to leave with him to the beach cabin for a few days. My emotions are rumblings of faraway thunder, eclipsed by the lightning bolt urgency of others. You can't leave *alone*; no one told you that you could love anyone so much. You're going to gather up what's yours and go home.

But I'd made not only a decision but a promise—and so I leave with my loving and forgiving dad, with my empty arms and heart.

Some people were less than kind about my decision. Many thought I should be a single mother, when as a young student I had no way in which to provide. It would be a two-job, no-father kind of life that didn't properly care for a child. If I left school, all I could probably get—after our largest local employer's current lay-offs in the area—would have been a minimum wage job; even less of a future for us. The option of living off public assistance, suggested by others, was never considered. Surprisingly, many were quite vocal that I should have had an abortion, and someone even verbally vilified me for "giving your kid away like it was a puppy"—such harsh, hurtful words.

But my decision was as difficult as anything I have ever done in my life. Any such decision is; and for people to openly judge mine was a cruelty that only honed my pain to razor sharpness.

16

Be Wary of the River

I woke to the sound of pouring rain, my family's house mostly empty as I didn't want a lot of people around right now. I needed to get up and get back to school; I'd already missed too many classes after I gave birth. But right now, all I could do was sit here and think, and cry.

The rain washes clean, but it as well leaves its mark. Marks that will not fade until further rain falls, filling that which was dry.

One summer, while my parents were away for a few hours, I defied orders to stay home with my brother, and jumped into the back of a car to go to the river—to swim with my friends, to erase the sticky hot chains of being a teen with a curfew. The warm air was like a balm. Fireflies flirting with twilight; the wind rippling my hair along with the summer pines; the sound almost that of silence. I looked up hoping to see a thunderstorm erupt, unknown power in the atmosphere that would only be washed away with the rain. Water cleansing the earth.

It was a small hatchback type car with two doors and a tiny

back seat. We were at a local swimming hole popular with teens; the car parked on an embankment pointed toward the water. I'd been forbidden to do anything other than extracurricular activities until my parents returned that night. But I didn't listen. It was innocent: no alcohol, just some kids, inner tubes, and some water—but still, I wasn't to come down here without my parents knowing where I was.

My friends were up front playing with the radio, forgetting to put the car in park. I was alone in the back, trying to get out of my shorts and T-shirt as my swim suit was on underneath, ready to hit the water as soon as we were out. My head was down and I had no sensation of movement. All I remember is an abrupt *bump bump bump* pushing me forward into the seat. And then the car went down that brief embankment into the water.

They say when you think you are going to die your life flashes before your eyes. Not true—all you see is water, and even before it touches your body your movement is slowed as if running a nightmare's marathon through it. My friends were out before the hood was completely underwater. The water hissed at the windshield like a really pissed off cat, and I pulled away out of instinct, anxious to protect my limbs. I was in the back, trapped by the seat. I'd either get over and out or I'd drown, it was as simple as that. The windows had been rolled down, an escape even if it provided a way for the water to say hello sooner. I clambered over the seats, got into the front and moved toward the window as the water pushed me away. One of my friends grabbed my arm to help pull me up and out and then accidentally let go of me—and I was headed downstream, vulnerable as a leaf.

There was no real chance that I'd drown at this point. The water was not that cold, there were no rapids, and I'm a strong swimmer. But try telling that to the fear. Pull, I told my arms. My arms obeyed, and I broke through the current and headed toward the shore—the vain instant of solid ground underfoot, touching me and then receding again, leaving me to flounder. But the water was not all that deep nor all that swift, and the shore was within reach. We gathered there, staring, stunned, other motorists around, as water dripped through my eyes like tears. The car was submerged. No one was hurt. It hit me then. Not how close we had come, not that the little Pinto at the bottom of the river probably wouldn't buff out.

What hit me was: "I'm going to be grounded for a YEAR."

It was only a month, not a year, and for that I am grateful; but a lesson was learned. Take no chances with the cold, precious waters. The river is wider than you think. On the mantle at home are some photos, including a couple of my mom. Thinking of her that night, I remembered all the things I was warned about. Don't swim for an hour after you eat. Don't stay in the water during a thunderstorm. *Be wary of the river that looks so cool and inviting, for that is the one in which you will drown.*

Thunder rumbled as I stayed silent, still hearing Mom's voice in my head and responding in kind. "I'll be careful next time, Mom, promise." Drops fell from the sky: salty, dense, leaving wet trails down my cheeks. The water rushed down—affirmation, promise, the healing power of cleansing rain.

17

Waiting in Silence

I stayed living in my family home for a few more months, getting back to school and returning to work only a few days after giving birth. Tuition was expensive and my dad believed in putting yourself through school, though he helped with food and books.

I brought nothing home from the hospital, even as I left something there—not a baby but something you could have lived your entire life with, without ever having known it was inside of you.

I know where my daughter is, and with whom; but my word is my honor and I promised not to get close. She has the option to contact me if she wishes when she turns of age, but if she doesn't? That, as they say, is that.

I gave my word. I will respect her choice if she never wishes to meet me, to know anything of me beyond words from her parents of "you were adopted." There is nothing to do now but go back to my life and try not to notice that when I stop to think if she is safe from harm, my breath catches as if there is no air; and I am going to have to learn to either not worry about her every moment or live without breathing.

So it is as if she's fixed in that moment; forever an infant, the walls of that hospital, the door to that room, fleeing away— leaving just her image immobilized within a tear, inviolate in innocence, forever safe from harm and alteration.

It's the only way I can sleep at night, as for the next eighteen years I wait for that phone to ring.

18

Empty Spaces

Late December, 1980-something. My daughter would be four years old, I thought to myself as I tucked a pair of jeans from earlier days into a box for Goodwill. I was at my dad's helping him organize some closets as he and my new stepmom continued to integrate her possessions into a house still full of the artifacts of our childhood.

I don't need the closet space in my childhood bedroom. I keep some clothes here for when I visit, but that is about it. Living as a pilot, I'm seldom in one place long enough to accumulate a lot of things: making lots of friends in the air, with a husband I met while traveling and married within a few months; too quickly some said, knowing my history of heartache.

Dad told me not to, saying only: "He's not what he seems to be." I didn't listen, determined that I was going to be happy without thinking the "how" completely through. But it was my choice; and for better or worse I was sticking it out, keeping my regrets to myself and not worrying Dad and my brother about them.

Looking through my closet, I realize I've probably the smallest collection of clothes of any woman I've ever met. There are dark blue suits, worn only for interviews or funerals; a single dress and pair of heels. Some easy-to-wash, -dry, or -burn clothes for hard work; jeans and such for play. I have two pairs of boots, sneakers, and a sensible pair work shoes that look like something Mickey Mouse would wear but in which I don't have to worry about an aircraft tool dropping and breaking a toe.

I view shopping for clothes somewhere along the lines of getting a root canal. But it's said clothes make the man, or woman. From our christening outfit to our burial outfit, something special is to be selected even if you're not in a position to actually care. Even the Bible has its own fashion standards: white linen for the resurrected or the angels, sackcloth and ashes for penitence and mourning. Priests wore robes of purest linen while Job's flesh was covered with tears.

Our scars tell our stories, not what we wear.

A fashion magazine has never graced my table, though I've thumbed through one at the hair salon for lack of anything else to read. I remember the one magazine that would post photos of "fashion don'ts" of real people, not models, wearing something the editors deemed unfashionable—the person's eyes covered with a black box like a gift from the executioner, the blindfold blocking out your last view, which is someone laughing at you.

When I was in sixth grade, there was this one little girl who wore a different outfit every day for weeks on end, with shoes and accessories to match. I had five or six dresses sewn by my mom. Beautifully made actually, but still homemade, for which this girl made fun of me at every opportunity; words hurled like fists, invisible bruises blossoming under fabric. I remember one day vividly, when a cheap mustard yellow purse I got to try and "accessorize" with was ripped out of my hand by her, held up for group ridicule as she and the popular girls ran off, leaving me there flapping in the wind like a lone shirt on a line. That was the only time in my life that something like clothing mattered so much to me, and I was glad now that my days away from home were spent in a uniform.

We all know about such girls, for they don't change as they age, resting in coiled balls of fur and insecurity, just waiting to show their claws to the weak before the weak realize they are not powerless at all. Now I just pity them; back then it simply hurt. But the torment didn't last long as junior high was in my future and I would be going to a different school soon.

I wore dresses much longer than others when the dress code was relaxed, but by the time I was sixteen I pretty much lived in Levi's, "waffle stompers" or sneakers, and turtlenecks, purchased cheaply. As girls we teased our friends going to the Catholic school about having to wear uniforms, fashion being about choice even as we wore almost identical clothing to school each day.

No one wore dresses anymore except to the prom, that night when parents would spend money they didn't want to on clothing you'd only wear once. Except my household. If I wanted a prom dress I'd be doing some extra babysitting. A lot of it. And I did. I had this fairy-tale dress of pale blue and white, off-the-shoulders but with a sheer shawl that covered them. I wore it with my long red hair curling down my back, fingers nervously plucking at the fabric as I waited for my date—who did not show. He didn't call, there was no emergency or accident. He simply stood me up. Dad watched as I waited and waited, the tears not coming until it was almost nine o'clock, the silent doorbell like a fist through a wall. I went to my room and ripped off the long dress, not caring if I damaged it; feeling as Job did, rending and tearing what I'd been promised, in my lamentation.

But there were other dresses in happy colors; there were pep sweaters, and handkerchiefs fragranced with perfume and stained with tears. There were thick winter coats dusted with snowballs, and brightly colored swimsuits that leaped from rocks into the river, suspended in the air like jewels tossed away. Then there were graduations, bell bottoms, and uniforms; the stiff fabric that shielded us from cold, the soft cotton lace of a young woman's nightgown on which a broken sonnet was etched in blood.

Now there are things in my closet that mean nothing except to me, draped on hangers or wrapped in plastic. There's a candy striper smock from the hospital, adorned with pins that show the hundreds of hours Mom spent there. There's an ancient but warm and fuzzy pink bathrobe; and a dress I wore my first day of kindergarten that Mom carefully wrapped and hung up.

I wondered what my daughter wore on her first day of kindergarten. Stop it, I tell myself, knowing where she likely lives a temptation I have to keep at bay, as I promised she would only meet me when she was grown. Driving by her house now only to get a glimpse would be a violation of more than just trust, that of a promise. I got back to work, shoving those thoughts deep into dusty boxes where they would best stay for now.

In another closet are my dad's military uniforms—still standing stiffly at attention years later. There's a blue shirt, my brother Allen's shirt that brings about the most wistful of smiles. There is a sweater that was my mother's. She left it draped on the chair when she left, where it remained for weeks as if Dad expected her to walk in again, healthy and whole. I try to picture it being worn but cannot; the garment lying flat, still beautiful but one-dimensional; as if painted upon canvas in which there is a tear.

There is a set of camouflage coveralls, worn but clean, simply waiting. I recall the last morning I wore them, on an annual deer hunt to put meat into the freezer for the long winter. I remember the eastern sky turning to primrose, then red with the firing of that first weapon; two of us walking in, whispers no louder than the silent dawn itself. The darkness seemed alive, God's breath biting at the back of my neck, raising goosebumps under the weight of my clothing. The blood surged, ran hotter, Pentecostal flames licking up my legs as we chased the sound of our blood into the tree line.

That night we donned stiff jeans and shirts softened by the

hands of a hundred washes, and we prepared a drink, an amber hallelujah pouring from a shot glass while out on the railing the coveralls hung waiting for another season of need. So many good memories there in that faded garment that still smells faintly of gunpowder and wood smoke; scents that to this day remind me of Allen.

Although I had little regard for fashion as a statement of our worth or need, I recognized something from the bits and pieces of clothing that were around me: what clothes we've possessed and retained are a chronicle, a story, a visual summation of small pieces of our lives.

As I worked first in my childhood closet and then my brother's, there were bits of clothing—some mine, some Allen's, getting organized, making our own memories. A pillowcase lay across the chair like a lover's shirt; Dad's dog made a nest of sweaters there on the floor, hoping not to be noticed. The clothing of two lives was strewn about in happy disarray, shoes and shirts and hats, and paper like a captain's log scattered, missing a few entries but for silken laughter. Half of the stuff didn't match, some didn't fit anymore, but I didn't care; bury me in the fabric of this place where I was once happy.

I took down a box from the shelf, the leaves blowing past the window reminding me of winter and of needed warmth as I headed out for a walk. My coat was years old; the hand-knit hat, my gloves, and my socks did not match. Outside in my home town someone aimed a camera, taking a picture of the new café, but framing me instead. I laughed and wondered if they would print it with a black box over my eyes and the words *Fashion Don't!* I don't mind, for of value to me is not what we wore on our backs but what we carried with us: our faith and our hopes as strong as stiff boots, as delicate as old lace.

19

Carrying On

Life, as the cliché says, does go on.

I had a busy life, having long ago donned the whole starched-uniform thing to see the world as a pilot. There was lots of travel between brief trips to home, but I still tried to make as much time to meet up with my big brother Allen as I could.

He was in the Navy, and opportunities for us both to meet up were limited; but we made the best of them even if it meant my flying in near where he was and renting a car to make the rest of the trip. Sometimes I'd swing by to see Dad before heading back to work or my own home so many miles away.

It was sometimes a lot of time on the road, but Dad's driving wasn't so great that I wanted him on a major interstate to pick me up at the airport, though he did great around town.

Allen had a new son now to add to his family. Though my visits weren't frequent, we cherished these times together; little had changed between us since when we were children. I was still childless, probably for the best the way my life had worked out; but I loved seeing my brother's two kids.

I always went for the same rental car agency, and I tried to go for a *big* vehicle, as there is nothing more unsettling than looking up at the undercarriage of a log truck—some of the logs secured by what looks like dental floss—on a rain-slicked highway.

The rental place I go to out west always has some chipper person who asks, "What brings you here?" I know they're just trying to be friendly, most people getting to them worn-out after flying long distances. That would render anyone cranky, especially a particular redhead whose suitcase went MIA—who now envisioned having to buy something to wear at the only store by Dad's, a big box mart with a ladies department full of outfits the size of tank parachutes.

So I wasn't in a particularly good mood, and besides: they just saw me two weeks ago after Dad had some minor surgery, during which I made more than one trip. And still they wanted to know what brought me here.

The next time they asked, even though I was just there a couple weeks ago, I gave them my sweetest smile and responded with:

"*Contract hit.* I'll be needing something with a large trunk."

The rental agent as usual didn't miss a beat, saying "That's nice, you want to upgrade to a full size then?"

There's a lot we do for family, but it helps when someone upgrades you in the process.

20

Shelter in Place

The next few years went by quickly; and over time there was a slight shift, an almost imperceptible change in my memory—and I could finally go to sleep without the occasional tears over a child who would be in her teens now.

I was still married—traveling a great distance for those times I worked, with lots of obligations on the small farm when I was home. I'd like to say I was happy there, but I wasn't. Looking back, I realize I got married so quickly to get back something I had lost—and you can't do that. There is no shelter in that, and shelter was what I had been seeking.

In those first years after the adoption, I literally flung myself out into the sky as often as I could. For the sky was my shelter. It was not a place free from danger. There's induction icing, geese without transponders, and gusts of wind that can come from nowhere; and if you're in the wrong piece of airspace, sometimes there's gun fire. But it was an environment in which I'd tested my mettle. Once you've landed on a strip of gravel 100 miles from another human—in a valley full of bears, no radio signal, no help, just a wrench, some food, and a firearm on your hip because of said bears—just because you had to pee, some things just don't seem all that scary.

Perhaps someday after I retire I will jot down these specific flying memories; but looking back it on it now, decades past my early career, I can only think back on the lessons they gave me back in the time when I needed them—not just for the air, but for life. You learn about chances taken; what you are comfortable with, what you are not. You learn about options. As a pilot those options can keep you safe and renew your faith. Not a blind faith that all will be well—that feeling has been the death of more than one airman—but a tentative faith that gives us the courage to venture onward. You have the knowledge that nothing is fixed, and the blessed understanding that as long as you are breathing and that old Pratt & Whitney engine is humming along, anything is possible.

I got my love of airplanes from my favorite uncle who worked as a senior engineer for Boeing. Uncle Rich traveled around the world, taking Aunt Marion with him as they weren't able to have kids of their own. Their small house was filled with the unique: beautifully sublime pieces of oriental wood and glass, exotic smells, and book after book of amazing adventure and history. He also came home with more than one airplane model.

Aunt Marion and Uncle Rich took Allen and me under their wings as if we were their own, with my parents' understanding and blessing of the close relationship. From what little I heard whispered there had been a number of miscarriages but no successful pregnancy. Aunt Marion was Dad's sister, and Uncle Rich was Mom's little brother. They grew up playing together, and like my mom and dad they fell in love and married.

We were an essential part of their lives, and we spent a great deal of time with our parents at their little house, their tending to us and loving us as if we were their own. If something had happened to my parents, they would have become our parents, it was simple and understood and as fixed as stone.

Allen and I saw the door on one of our first visits there: a hefty airtight-looking piece of sheet metal that covered steps leading down to a small cement-lined room. We'd heard about it from the neighborhood kids, and we wanted to check it out. As we took a cautious glance inside we saw lights, an emergency generator, some water, and canned food. We'd heard about the shelters after the Cuban Missile Crisis; I knew the stories well. Yes, if *anyone* on the block was going to have a real Cuban Missile Crisis bomb shelter, it was going to be our Uncle Rich and Aunt Marion.

That bomb shelter became our hideaway, our fort, our playground. We'd creep down the stairs and lay on the floor, taking in the mysterious earthy smell, the eerie greenish glow of the single outlet casting dark shadows on the wall. Down in the dark and the quiet we'd talk in little trickling bursts of secret murmurings, conversations among best friends, fellow survivors. Our only light would be a small flashlight, the beam shining on the pallet of supplies we lay on, half in the light, half in the dark, the beam on our legs like moonlight.

After Uncle Rich died suddenly a short time later, Aunt Marion stayed in the house. Allen and Dad took care of any yard work or needed repairs to the place, taking my aunt where she needed to go; for although she traveled the entire world both with Uncle Rich and afterwards alone, she never learned to drive.

When I saw Aunt Marion, it was always at Dad's house for all the usual holidays. I talked to her often, but I never went back to her place after my uncle died because we always met at Dad's. In the summer of 2001 she died suddenly, and it was after her memorial service that I went back to her house for the first time in years.

I never noticed how small it really was—only 600 square feet, the yard a postage stamp of tired grass. My aunt and uncle never wanted anything bigger; their passion was travel and that's where their road lay, their time and income. In that inevitable failing of those who haven't shaken hands with death, I thought our time together was infinite. Each year I thought about making an extra trip to visit her house; but before I knew it I was grown and the mysterious dark bunker was a distant memory, though Aunt Marion never was. When my family said our last goodbye to her home that week as it went for sale, I saw the closed shelter doors. I hadn't been down there in over twenty-five years. It was still small and dark; clean, snug, and dry. Then I noticed the tiny washer and dryer, the cans of food, the laundry basket. I looked at my brother. "This was her laundry room," Allen said, where she'd had some extra space for her small home. The "bomb shelter" was nothing more than my aunt and uncle's post-war laundry and cellar with a few supplies in case of storm, a special-built little extra space for their tiny home on its tiny lot.

The bomb shelter story was simply a childhood myth, spread through the years by neighbor kids and embraced as something uniquely strange and foreign to our stable and prosperous life in the '60s. Ours was one of the first generations to live with the concept of instant global annihilation; yet as children, a generation who had never directly experienced war, we only thought it cool, a sci-fi-like fable.

I think about those early days as I arrive to the flight line, not just for duty but to get away from the thoughts swirling around my head; choices made, beds made. With me goes simply a uniform cap and a small photo holder thin as a credit card to tuck into my uniform pocket. In it is a faded photo taken quickly through a window—of a beautiful little ginger-haired baby.

Today this plane is my shelter. It's the soft-throated roar of an engine that even as it ceases there remains in the immediate air an echo of where I wish to go. It's the wheels breaking free of the earth, like a hand lifted above the profound desolation of the past, a supplication to the sky. It's the glint of the sunrise ahead, the smile of daybreak hinting at upcoming wonders, a lover's smile of promise. My craft surrounds me, it's tangible and honest and real; and if I care for it and treat it right it will not fail me. It's an affirmation of trust in a web of fabric and wood. When I look up I see only light, and when I look around I see only what is necessary for my happiness, nothing more.

When I'm aloft I don't know who I was or who I will be, I am simply there with the element of infinity that is the horizon. I know that I am alive. I know that I love.

I don't need to know anything else, moving forward into the immortality of a small piece of time, of all that my mind is capable of and my spirit can want. Risk is but a novelty that drives me to excel, to take control of my craft, of my future, and my life as I find comfort in the shifting boundaries between earth and the heavens. It's an escape and a shelter, as essential to my spirit as the ocean-like smell of the air and the wave of my comrades with me as I waggle my wings, leaving formation. Away to my future, to a secret place of joy that no one can steal from me.

Away to my sheltering sky.

21

Words Taking Shape

As I sat at the airport yet again waiting for a flight to my dad's for a few days, I was glad I had brought a book to read. You're never alone if you have a book to read, I thought to myself. I enjoyed these trips even if they only happened a couple of times a year for a few days. On these visits Allen and I would have cribbage wars, and my stepmom would fix something up in the kitchen using Mom's old cookbooks which she thoughtfully took good care of.

On the road I usually stop in a bookstore if there is one around. So many books. The bargain books are generally entertaining in and of themselves, leaving me wondering what prompted some people to pen such thoughts to paper. I chuckled to myself as I thought of a few titles for books that would instantly land in the bargain bin:

Living Life Chocolate-Free

My Little Ponies—Track Bets and You

Bouncing Betty and the Bucket of Moonshine—A Nancy Drew Mystery

Get Off My Leg!! A Beginner's Guide to Dog Training

But good books have been part of my life since early childhood. Allen and I were lucky to have two parents who exposed us to books and music. Learning and discovery were elemental to them, and reading and words became a quiet necessity of my life. *Charlotte's Web, The Wind in the Willows, A Child's Garden of Verse*, and my all-time favorite, *Grimm's Fairy Tales*.

Books were my portal to comfort during those inevitable awkward moments of growing up, a way of immersing myself in the world of an author. As a child, books helped me grow, stretching my mind even further. And through books and written words came friendships. I'd talk about what I read with my classmates, telling snippets of stories and passing around dog eared copies of Asimov and Heinlein and Niven and Herbert. We'd gather over our lunches, laughing about a recent share, Philip K. Dick's *Do Androids Dream of Electric Sheep?* We'd sit until a teacher made us go back to class, voices raised in excitement for the vast reaches out there, limitless possibilities that we on the cusp of adulthood believed existed.

With that the world opened up to me. I started recording what I saw in it in small notebooks—ink drawings, loose photos added onto their pages, a scrapbook of my life recorded for eternity with nothing more than an old Mont Blanc pen and a camera.

Opening one of those old notebooks at random, now a quote jumps out at me:

> Words dazzle and deceive because they are mimed by the face. But black words on a white page are the soul laid bare.
>
> —Guy de Maupassant

"Soul laid bare." The sense of vulnerability in those three words is beyond reach. From these recorded pages has come my own story—tales of the possibilities of life, my soul laid out for you to read. I believe in the magic hidden in people and things; and the words in these notebooks brings it out into the light.

For me reading and writing are not just intellectual but embracive. I love the way the spine of a book or notebook feels in my hands. A book has an aesthetic charm of endless possibilities as I take in the smell of ink, the texture of a page as my fingers gently turn it. Between 1850 and the late 1980s books were printed on acidic paper. Conservators now can't keep up with the costly restoration. It has been said that millions of books in thousands of libraries the world over will be lost when their pages finally disintegrate into dust, leaving us only to mourn the loss of the words.

I love blank notebooks. To me, it's hard to think of anything that represents the clean slate of opportunity more than a pristine, empty notebook. Smythson of Bond Street has bound ones with delicate blue pages that look like the airmail paper my parents wrote to one another on during the War. The paper is so thin that the ink bleeds through, yet the pages still chronicle the experiences that are in danger of being lost by the errant click of a mouse. In today's evolution of the tools of our expression, we've lost the very things we can hold on to. Things that can still gather dust and be passed on to a child, to a lover, to history—even if two hundred years from now the paper and the one I wrote the words for are only dust and starlight.

Tonight I sit alone and in quiet.

I don't read a lot of popular fiction, I prefer nonfiction and history. I like reading about the long ago. I know more about my own life when I learn about the past. It's a sense of perspective on days full of people who killed, tortured, struggled, and suffered; agonizing about things that were of the utmost importance to them; working and living for reasons that may well be the same as ours. Now they've been gone some 500 years, and all that is left to us is the essence of their lives. To me history is more than a story, more than a book. It's the life and the heart and soul of ages long ago. It's the ultimate myth and inevitably ambiguous; but I do believe that, in the words of Lord Bolingbroke, "History is philosophy teaching by example and also by warning." Someone else said, "History not read is like ammunition not used." And without reading, for me at least, the past is silence and the future is haze.

So for these many reasons I hate being stuck somewhere without a book, a notebook, or a laptop with which to record my thoughts. Let the weather play God with my itinerary, let them send me to Elbonia. I've been stuck in places where my luggage did not arrive at the same time I did and the only written word I could find in English was a ferry schedule for the River Styx. I don't care where I am; I simply need something to read and something to write on. Words in reserve, a buttress against the whims and dubiety of travel, of growing up, of life itself.

But now my writings have taken on another meaning, for I'm writing for my daughter. For her these stories of my youth; of this time here, now; of the lifetime of years I did not know her. Perhaps she and I will never meet. Perhaps all she will have of me after I am gone will be these words. Perhaps she won't read them at all.

But the stories will be there, claimed or not.

I have a new little notebook in my suitcase. When I removed the protective wrapping, its crackling sound awakened something in me. I stroked the oilskin cover for the first time, my future turning before me as I snapped open the elastic band to flip through the pristine pages, dreams waiting to burst out onto them. The pages were too perfect; it was almost hard to make the first mark upon their clean, fresh landscape. But with the thought of a child and the small touch of a child's hand against my face I began; splaying the words on lasting paper before they were lost in the ether. Words that would be bequeathed to the page before they were forgotten. Words that, though not spoken, would take a corporeal shape in my heart whenever I closed my eyes, even as they themselves slumbered between the closed cover that became their hiding place.

22

Free Willy

My family always seemed to have a dog around the house. Some were rescue dogs, and one was purebred, obtained from a reputable breeder. After I moved out, Dad got a little rescue mutt of unknown origin that resembled a mop but was the sweetest, smartest little thing.

After I got married and had moved far away from home I had a dog or two, though being on the road so much they were less mine and more my large extended family's. These dogs migrated between our farmhouse and my husband's family members who lived just down the private road, separated only by a few acres.

One of the dogs was a Lab, a hunting dog who lived for ducks and ponds. I'd have preferred he not do that: there were gators further to the south, and large snapping turtles lurking in the water could do some serious damage to an animal. The one dog that had no desire to get anywhere near the water was Sammy, our rescued Husky.

Sammy wasn't a hunting dog, he was a shedding dog. I once got so much hair off him in one brushing that I filled up a large trash bag with it. I later found it taped to the steering wheel of our old Buick with the note "driver's side hair bag."

But one thing Sammy would retrieve, and constantly: turtles. Box turtles, to be precise. I wasn't sure where he got them, but figured probably from around the pond in the back. At least once or twice a month he'd be at the back door with a box turtle in his mouth, unharmed, waiting for a treat because of this great gift he had brought me. Box turtles have a movable hinge on their lower shell that allows them to retract inside their armor and then completely close up leaving no flesh exposed; but I was afraid Sammy's sharp teeth might still do some damage. So I'd gently take the turtle from him and go out to the back field to let it go.

But one day he kept going back and back and bringing me the same turtle. I was afraid he'd hurt it; so the last time, I decided to just take the turtle back to his home, where the dog couldn't get him. *The pond.*

I walked out back, the turtle cradled motionless in my hands as if he were made of glass. The sun was high and hot, contemplating us sleepily like a large somnolent yellow cat, and I could smell the water. As I got to the water's edge, I lobbed him out into the center of the pond.

Time almost stopped as he hung there for a moment, motionless and without physical weight, then finally giving over to time and gravity and descending in a perfect arc into the center of the deep pond.

Free Willy!

Sploosh!!! His shell closed up, he sank to the bottom like a stone, and with a few air bubbles he was free.

I got home that night and my brother-in-law came over a tractor, and I told him what I had done. He started laughing so hard he cried.

Apparently box turtles are *land* turtles, and though they might gently paddle a bit in a shallow warm snippet of water, swimming up from a dive to the depths was not in their repertoire.

I sent Mr. Turtle to his doom.

I felt terrible, *but hoped he at least enjoyed the brief flight.*

I couldn't fault Sammy. He was just trying to please his human mom. Adopting him had been a good thing to do when I found him at a shelter, as he helped take away some of the quietness of the house. I'd been unable to conceive again, and the quiet in the house was sometimes unbearable until broken by a joyous bark. Sammy didn't make up for the quiet, but he was still a balm to my spirit, one of those souls we bring into our lives for a reason that is often not obvious at the time.

23

Tracks to Nowhere

I wonder if my daughter ever thinks of me. The years are going by way too quickly, yet not quickly enough. There is a part of me that wishes I could fast forward to her being an adult so that I can share in all those years I missed.

Yet when I was a child I rarely thought of my origins—happy and safe with Mom and Dad, I was thinking of little else.

When Mom died I made an attempt to find out more about my biological parents, more from a standpoint of medical history. Allen had no such interest, not wishing to know if there was a ticking time bomb contained within his web of flesh and bone.

I knew my birth date, obviously; but I also knew the name of the hospital and the time of my birth. So I quietly searched, checking out every website out there that had adoption registries, looking for anyone, parent, sibling, *someone* who wondered if I was alive.

Insert sound of crickets.

There was nothing, no records, no family. No one was looking for me, and no one wanted to be found.

I wonder: Does my daughter think of me there in her room, looking into her eyes in the mirror, wondering where they got their shape or color? Does she wonder if I am OK, or am I just some tale told before bedtime to be forgotten when she falls asleep?

I look out the window to a sullen southern sky. I hadn't planned on being here; the announcement that we were moving a thousand miles to help on the family farm made within days after we married. There was no discussion, I had no say in the matter. My rental home was vacated, most of my possessions given away. All we took was what would fit into a small moving trailer. But I'd have family, I told myself—finding out quickly that simply because you bear a name does not make you belong.

Behind the house ran railroad tracks. I remember the first week there, my first experience in a land where tornadoes regularly tap on the door, tossing mobile homes around like a two-year-old having a tantrum in the grocery store. I had been left alone for a couple of days, watching the sky with a pilot's eye and not liking what I saw.

On the TV one night came the tornado warning. Of course I had no clue what county I was in, the move having been so sudden. I had always heard that a tornado sounds like a freight train. As one of the family dogs and I huddled in the living room, fierce wind pounding on the window, I heard it—the sound of a train. Grabbing mattress and dog I fled to the bathtub and prepared to die. The sound faded, as did the wind. Looking out all I could see were a few small branches down, but that was it.

The next morning I went for a walk, only to discover the railroad tracks. That had been no tornado but simply the ten p.m. eastbound train. It had sounded like a train because it *was* a train.

Today, years later, there is no train on that same spot of ground—no forlorn whistle flung out upon a brooding sky, no boxcars going anywhere just waiting to be filled. I had hoped to see it, to catch that train as it flew by to somewhere, caught in a moment between ecstasy and agony, the years flying by with the color of sound.

But today there is no train. There are just thoughts of rails and ties not yet laid down, tracks that might never exist. There is an empty house with a small room that was going to be a nursery, now just full of boxes. There is only this solitary woman, left to wonder if the aloneness will be all she will know.

As I go back into the house to start packing my things, the crickets begin their song.

24

Fellow Travelers

When we our betters see bearing our woes,
We scarcely think our miseries our foes.
Who alone suffers, suffers most in the mind,
Leaving free things and happy shows behind.
But then the mind much sufferance doth o'erskip
When grief hath mates, and bearing fellowship.

—*King Lear*, William Shakespeare

When I'm traveling, I'm constantly watching the little things around me to see if something is slightly out of kilter. I think it's part of being a pilot, noting how the world changes around you in oh-so-small and subtle ways. Yet there are moments in my day when I'm privileged to observe simple every-day human interaction without the risk of personal involvement. Events which to most people would appear inconsequential, but to a lone observer they are infused with a sense of poignancy so touching and intense that you can't help but take it home with you.

One such event I recently witnessed could have been discarded as trivial to someone focused on the rush to catch a flight or to get home to a loved one, likely missed altogether. I had a flight to someplace for something routine I didn't want to do right now, other things on my mind. Perhaps it was just my over-emotional state lately that colored the event to raise it above that of the mundane. Having dealt with such emotions in the past I could recognize them in others. At any rate, what I witnessed on a typical day on the run, a day stretched longer than a country road, still stays in my mind.

It was a small section of the airport concourse that is usually quiet and empty except for the squeals of children during day-time—playing on some plastic play equipment, bustling about with the inexhaustible energy characteristic of only the very young while their travel-weary parents get a few precious moments to simply breathe. I sat down to make a phone call, only to have the person I was trying to reach say, "Let me call you back in just a minute."

Then across from me a young woman, still a teen, sat down in one of the empty plastic chairs. I noticed her because she had the same coloring as my daughter did as a baby, strawberry blond hair and blue eyes. She had a book bag from a state college and was dressed cleanly and neatly in the latest fashion, holding the book bag along with her purse. Like the rest of us, she looked thrilled to have finally escaped the aircraft after being wedged in a too-small seat for too long.

I really should have minded my own business—but I was waiting for my phone call to be returned before I went down the escalator that takes you to baggage claim and out to freedom, into the area of no phone reception. So I watched her, one leg drawn up, holding her arm up to her chest, as she excitedly got out her cell phone with a smile and a longing in her movements that touched my heart. Probably going to call her boyfriend to tell him she was on the ground and ready to be picked up. I moved down another section of seats to give her a bit of privacy for her conversation. So although I could not hear the words spoken, I couldn't help but notice her reaction as the conversation became softly animated, then pleading; her hand moving as she spoke, a futile and formal expression of all promise. Then apparently a dial tone as the blood rushed from her lips mid-sentence. I've seen enough of life to recognize a girl whose heart has just been broken.

She sat there, stunned, while outside the sky thickened into a dark blanket with only a few rays of light shining through, like holes punched into dense cloth. Then the tears began as she put her hand over her mouth as if to hold in the sound, her disbelieving betrayed eyes darting about like small frightened birds, afraid that she might be noticed. The concourse was almost empty, a gathering solitary thunderstorm and I her only witnesses. We all just sat there, all alive and all alone, still, and seemingly disinterested.

I had this sudden almost uncontrollable urge to get up and go to her to tell her it'd be OK, at least offer her a tissue and a comforting mom-like smile, and a ride somewhere if she needed it. Women can do that with a touch, with a word. Non-threatening, we can sometimes convey a heart while totally bypassing the brain. But I didn't move. After all, this was none of my business and she and I both likely knew "ride with stranger" is never a good idea. I tried to convince myself to mind my own business, whilst somehow I was unwittingly absorbing all her pain and loneliness.

She sat there crying for a while on that solitary seat in her land of tears, with a melancholy aura radiating from a face that had just aged ten years. Then as the tears dried, she quickly got up with her book bag and onto the escalator with small timid steps, holding on to the wall for support like a small child. I had this uneasy feeling of somehow failing to communicate with her—although it was not my affair—nevertheless; that life was still good and that the next day would dawn; and somewhere in her promising future there would be someone out there who would protect her, who would hurt deeply along with her if he ever made her cry.

But she was gone, probably through the terminal by now, disappearing into the gray wet dullness of a late evening rain shower. I sat there feeling frustrated and upset and could not even understand why. The event I had just witnessed was not earth-shattering. On a global scale, compared to the miseries and devastation of a world in conflict, the carnage and desolation caused by man and mother nature both on regular basis, this little melodrama was less than a quick blip on a radar. In the grand scheme of things it never happened. Why should it bother me?

But it did, for I had witnessed a fellow traveler on this life's journey in torment; and in spite of my naturally kind heart I did nothing to offer help, comfort, or just a friendly word. Yes, it was none of my business, really; but somehow as a fellow human being I knew it was and that I had failed. I believe that the distress of even one soul echoes in all of us. Whether you feel it touching you, or it passes you seemingly unnoticed in the disinterest of another busy day, no one is entirely free of the heartaches of the world.

As I walked through the terminal on my way out I looked and noticed other people, really noticed. A young mother placing her baby in a stroller and securing her in it with such care. A young man who stopped to help an old woman whose roller bag just tipped over. Though we may have not signed on for the job or even want the duty, we are all caretakers. I make my living by picking through the broken pieces of failure and poor choice, to aid the living by conferring with the dead; yet on this night I was as ineffective as any bystander waiting beyond the yellow tape, there only to look and not help.

Returning to my rental car in the bright gloom of a stormy summer night, the sadness of a stranger touched my heart. I thought of my daughter and hoped that when she was hurting there would be someone to comfort her, for I could not. As I prepared for bed, I softly sang a lullaby that would not be heard, singing her to sleep in this city that never sleeps.

As the words trailed off into the silence of my empty room, I realized that it had never stopped raining this night. After all, perhaps the skies do have the capacity to weep for even one small soul who aches.

25

Lessons from a Garage

They weren't frequent, but I loved those times I could fly out West to visit my family, even if only for a long weekend. Those weekends were rest, they were restoration. My brother Allen and I would end up in Dad's garage, working side-by-side on some project. The garage was shadowed by trees, and it was old and had little in the way of modern conveniences. But I liked it that way. It was a place where tools were old, wood was honed, metal was bent, and burnt offerings to British cars were offered to Lucas, Prince of Darkness (or Dimness, depending on your religious persuasion). It was easy to spend hours there without realizing it, the space between tasks still composing time; consisting of minutes that no longer ran straight ahead in diminishing allotment, but rather parallel between, like looping bands of wiring without apparent ending.

It was only when the light faded and our stomachs growled that we looked up and noted the time, setting down the tools, rendering the machinery mute as we returned to the house, a faint shadow against the steps in the fading sky.

Most of the neighbors were parked in the driveway, their garages full of stuff; boxes, bikes, lawn and exercise equipment, you name it. When I was a kid, it seemed most of our cars were actually *in* the garage. We had a dark green ranch house with a dark green Chevy Malibu in the garage. Outside at the front edge of the lawn was a huge tree that Mom loved, draping its branches over the driveway like a canopy, filling up the gutters with leaves every year.

Whenever I spent my vacation days visiting Dad, I seemingly always found a reason to visit the garage. There was always an extra freezer out there, full of an assortment of bundled cow and mysterious Tupperware labeled "brussels sprouts" or "creamed peas"—which we found out too late were actually cookies that Mom had squirreled away for church luncheons and baby showers knowing we wouldn't raid the "creamed peas." There was lefse from the Sons of Norway Bake Sale. There was always ice cream.

In the corner were Dad's and Allen's golf clubs; in front of them space where we used to park our bikes. My last one was that Huffy ten-speed that Dad so lovingly obtained and fixed up. I wasn't what I'd wanted, but it was much more because it was offered with quiet and undiluted love, the faithful care and attention that most people don't put into anything anymore. That was a lesson I may not have recognized then, but I do today.

The biggest decorative item in the garage was the tacky Mexican bull fighting picture Dad bought for his and Mom's first home, which was immediately banished to the garage. It joined a well-used dartboard and other works of fine art that found a home in Dad's "man cave."

Off to one side of the garage was a big work bench with cupboards built above for storage. Dad didn't use it much anymore but it had not changed, except for the calendar: always the smiling, buxom girl in shorts and a T-shirt or a swim suit, selling tools or beer.

In the shadows of the other side of the garage were deep storage cabinets where Dad stored all his fishing and outdoor gear. Everything was meticulously kept in place, even as the fabric of his old fishing net rotted; lying in wait with that spent but alert quality that aging things have—as if they doubted the absoluteness of their eventual discard, as if they would be necessary and needed tomorrow.

There's just a single garage door. There's probably a small dent in the bottom of it. When I was about eight years old, I tried to ride my bike at warp speed *into* the garage when the car was out and the door was partway up, planning on ducking, just not ducking enough. It knocked me clean off my bike, but no permanent damage was done, really (*twitch-twitch*). But the neighborhood no longer being the safe haven that it was, the windows that once brought in light are now covered with contact paper so not to let potential burglars peer in to see if anyone is home.

In the driveway there used to be a little VW Beetle, Mom's

official bug-out vehicle which later became my car. But the Chevy was always stored in the garage, except for those rainy weekends when we set up the Lionel trains there on large pieces of sheet plywood, spray painted green, sitting on trestles. Old Pringles containers were fastened underneath to hold the tracks, and we'd run the trains along frantic loops of track until our stomachs growled and the fading evening light illuminated them like silvered spider webs running off into the distance. Only then, on Sunday nights, were the trains put away amidst the other supplies.

When the weather was good Dad would work at his bench, while we'd get a bat and send a ball down the drive towards the road, into that conundrum of physics and aerodynamics that never failed to fascinate me. More than one go-cart was assembled out in the driveway with Dad's advice and more than a few of his tools.

As we got older the trains we played with were replaced by Allen's first car. He and his friends were forever tinkering with something they bought cheap to fix up. One day while I was hanging around just to be close to him, as he was changing the oil he handed me a wrench and said, "Let me show you how to do this." I asked, "Why?" His voice stopped for a moment, though his tone remained in the air like when the needle is lifted off an old record album by the hand of someone wondering if someone else hears the same music.

I was listening. He paused to wipe the sweat from his brow and said, with a steadiness that told me I needed to listen, "You need to learn how to do some of this yourself. I won't always be here, but you will always have yourself."

So as a young woman, Allen taught me how to change my oil and a tire, do a basic tune-up, and keep my car in running order. While my friends were frosting each other's hair more blond, I was putting Purple Horny Headers on my VW Bug (it was still a Bug, but you could hear me coming five blocks away) while we listened to an old transistor radio. I learned the safe handling of tools and what was used for what purpose, working together out in the garage as if our forms were joined by some mechanical arm. We'd work until my arms ached, fading light drowsing on the floor like a drop cloth, slowed down by fatigue but still in motion, still inevitable. Only when Mom, or later Dad, called us in to supper would we quit.

"You will always have yourself." Those words were salt and truth. Allen knew me better than I knew myself. To my dad I would always be his little girl to protect and to care for. But my brother recognized that I was not the type to be happy totally dependent on someone, fated to settle for flesh and bone durable enough to do battle for both of us while I stood in the shadows, inviolate bride of silence, doomed to fail. Allen saw it, though it was a while and some tears before I learned it for myself.

When I did, I knew what I had to do.

26

Wheels Turning

The nail swung as miles and miles were put under my wheels. The drive from the farm to my new life up north was a long one. The details of those end days of that early marriage aren't important, only what I took from them. I did not take many things with me; only some tools, clothes, and college textbooks that I thought I might need as was planning on going back to finish graduate school once I'd saved enough money.

There it was, with a small group of photos shoved into an envelope: a wedding photo. Why I couldn't throw it out is beyond me. I looked at the photo. As tall as I was, he towered over me—his muscled form looking quite uncomfortable in an off-the-rack suit. I stood in full virginal white, miles of lace and chiffon, my hands dutifully folded, and my long red hair covering my shoulders. I looked so very young, hopeful, and trusting. The fear and the flinching with sudden movement would come later.

I guess I looked beautiful; but my big green eyes revealed a deep sadness. I was still mourning a living child, and yet my

smile was flawless. I did not look like I'd spend ten years past-
ing that smile on my face. But I would. That pasted-on smile
began that night and continued for years as I fought to prove
that I was a good wife, a loyal wife. It was a losing battle no
matter what I did.

We swallow a lot to stay the course of work, of friendship, of
love; more than we expected and usually more than we should.
Money, history, familiarity, duty. These forces are powerful and
sometimes wear a mask that people mistake for a good reason.
But the reasons erode away at your soul and your self-esteem
like water against rocks.

We absorb like sponges the disappointment, wounding insults,
infidelity, and betrayal; and for some things, some people, the
endurance may well be worth it. For a time. And one day, while
walking along a trail with the first snow fall on the ground, you
know. And it's either going to be you or fate that steps in.

You remember the good parts. You hold on to the memories of
sheer moments of discovery, of hopes for a normal life; sweeping to the corner the later moments of pain and lies and needs
you could never meet. Moments that shattered like glass on
the clean surface of your life. You entered into the relationship
knowing he came with emotional and psychological baggage;
and you think you can fix them even as you're working on fixing yourself. As if the power of the fragile loves of youth could
shape something that's set into his core like a steel beam. But
you stay for family, for guilt—until the circumstances of your
suspect choice and your fears have defaced your picket fence

dream like a crazed graffiti artist. You stay out of misdirected love, thinking somehow that simply through will you can change the circumstances of how someone views the world, of how he views you.

As I settle into my new home as a now-single person, I place the photo deep inside a book I will never open again. Overhead a sound passes by—the somnolent gnashing crunch of tires meeting gravel. The sound moving away, dying, not to return. A sigh of release escapes from the depths of my being; or maybe it's the wind in the trees, shivering stalks against the sky. There have been tears; but they eventually slow to a quiet seeping of dreams against a pillow in the night; muffled resignation, undetectable during the day. It's not the first time I've experienced such days—ones that grow round and monotonous, life slowing to one of quiet acceptance.

I head out to explore the little town where I've found a place to set up home; a rural area outside of a big city, fields around and a body of water a stone's throw away. Along the path with me is a lady with her retriever, his nose to the ground seeking something with an integrity that as a human I can only admire. The air is cold. Clear. Sharp. Cutting as a knife to the landscape flayed and laid bare to the eye under the surgical light of a winter morning.

The cold restricts movement as it propels it, pushing us toward something that will warm us. The cold, like life, only accentuating that which we cannot sustain. You move forward or you will die.

27

Some Things Are
Best Left Silent

I was thinking of getting a dog to keep me company.

Dogs will always be my favorites; though certainly I've been around other pets either by association or adoption. But I needed to save some money for a proper house with a fenced yard first.

There was a snake. Not mine but belonging to a coworker's son who had built a herpetarium for his boa constrictor as part of a high school project. They went out of town for a weekend and I was asked to (1) water the plants and take in the mail and (2) feed the snake. I said, "OK, where's the Purina snake chow?" Uh-oh.

Apparently snakes like their food still alive. So I took the owner's directions to a pet store that sold feeder rodents. I hated to do it but I'd given my word. So I left to bring back a couple of mouse-like objects. I felt bad enough as it was. Having a barn cat to keep the mice down was one thing—but I was supposed to feed them live to a snake? I hate snakes. I felt worse and worse as I approached the house. It did *not* help that the small carrier the store had given me to transport the mice was shaped and painted like a little house with the lettering "Thanks for giving me a home."

The snake didn't buy into the Twinkie with two little almonds stuck to it for ears and a tail made out of a piece of licorice. It went hungry till the next day when the owner returned and the mice had "accidentally" escaped into a local abandoned barn. I do understand the need to eat and where food comes from; but knowing that snakes can safely go without food for a while, I just couldn't be party to what would not be a quick, clean demise.

I missed having a pet. A dog was going to have to wait a bit longer; but somehow I ended up with a bird for a couple of months while its owner did a short internship out of state. It was just a little cockatiel. They're like budgies on steroids, right? How much trouble could he be? He was a pretty personable little bird and easy cared for by others while I was in class or working. Cockatiels are smart and normally learn to talk. Not this bird. I had inherited a mute bird. I tried all the tricks, repeating words over and over, rewards, more repetition. Nothing. "No, no, he's not dead, he's, he's restin'! Remarkable bird, the Norwegian Blue, idn'it, ay? Beautiful plumage!" as Michael Palin famously used to say in *Monty Python's* "Dead Parrot Skit."

This bird was not "restin'," he just would *not* talk. Not even a "Hello."

My apartment was near the shores of a lake, which I enjoyed—it reminded me of the brief time I had rented a small houseboat. It wasn't a real boat, just a tiny bungalow on floats with a tiny kitchen, living room, and bath with shower. It also had a small windowed loft with a ladder going upstairs, where I had a mattress on the floor and could tuck myself in at night. I loved living out there on the only houseboat in the marina, enjoying the quiet and the lap of the waves against my little home. (We won't mention the time when two hippie girls were getting a bit tipsy on a boyfriend's boat docked out in the shallows while he was away, when I put on a *Creature from the Black Lagoon* mask, rowed out right at dusk, scratched on the hull, and pressed my face to the glass—making my escape as someone squealed and dropped a bottle of Chardonnay.)

But I was in the Midwest now, not the warmer waters of the West; and this lake near my apartment would likely freeze clear across in the winter. I had dusted off my pilot's wings and taken a new job flying for a private company part-time while I finished school. It was good to be out again, and my family was coming to visit soon.

It wasn't a big home but my family was happy to visit it as we grilled out on the small patio and toasted to better days ahead. The mute cockatiel was in high form, sitting on people's shoulders, walking across the room (he could fly, he just chose *not* to), getting fed some treats. Eventually everyone headed to bed with the exception of my brother. Allen stayed up with the bird perched on his shoulder and a selection of sports and probably not-safe-for-work cable TV.

With earplugs in, I slept like a log. In the morning I came out to a sleeping household and a strange voice. For my friend's cockatiel was back in his cage, proudly proclaiming at the top of his little bird lungs in a voice that sounded way too much like Allen's: "Nice ass!" Apparently, *someone* had been up late watching naughty vision.

The bird had learned his first and only words. I had a feeling his owner would be less than pleased.

28

Hearts of Glass

I have this blown glass vase on my shelf. It is round, not quite bowling ball shaped. Within its form, colors make up the swirling shapes of fish, and as the light shines on them they appear to swim. It weighs about twenty pounds and was my grandmother's as a young woman, surviving three generations.

Yet as strong as it is, I know that if I dropped it on the floor of my garage, it would shatter into a hundred pieces, schools of little glass guppies flip-flopping to every corner of the room as it broke.

Glass may be defined simply as a super-cooled liquid with a viscosity that for all practical purposes makes it a solid. Glass is rigid at ambient temperatures and soft or fluid-like at elevated temperatures. It is a substance whose exact definition is up for debate. In a broad sense, solids can be considered to be either crystalline or amorphous. Crystals have symmetrical and repeating patterns for the constituent atoms, sharp melting points, and cleave in preferred directions. Amorphous solids show none of these characteristics. The glass state is a category of the amorphous state and encompasses solids that may be softened by heating to viscous liquids, which revert to non-crystalline solids when cooled.

In its lifetime, when it's liquid glass is a solid that can be bent and molded, colored and crafted; but always in its finished form it is still subject to breaking.

You don't see glass soda bottles as often as you used to, cans having been found to be a cheaper and better medium in which to transport the contents. As kids we were only allowed soda pop on our vacation to my uncle's ranch. The rest of the time we had milk, water, and Kool-Aid. My vice of choice was Orange Crush in the tall glass bottle, so many consumed during that summer vacation that my lips seemed to be permanently stained light orange.

The bottles then became targets, blown into shining shrapnel out in a stone quarry as my mom keep proficient even if she was no longer the sheriff, then later teaching Allen and me how to safely and responsibly handle a firearm. We were from a long lineage of law enforcement and defense, the duties and responsibilities that came with that honed early, the mantle ours to take up only if it was our calling.

We would shoot until the ground dazzled with the bottles' remnants in the summer sun, pieces glinting like diamonds. The tiny fragments remained, not flattened by rain to valueless fragments of repudiation but sharp, waiting; still able to cut long after they were laid down into silence.

As children we didn't think that glass was composed partially of silicon dioxide in the form of quartz, which has some of the structural characteristics of diamonds. Unlike diamond, which has only tetravalent carbon arranged in interconnected six-membered rings, quartz has six-membered rings of alternating silicon and oxygen atoms. The oxygen atoms preclude forming the same structure as that found in diamond.

We knew nothing of that even as we neared adulthood. All we knew was that feeling of pulling the rifle up to our shoulder, taking aim under the tutelage of a parent, and watching that bottle shatter at the pull of a finger.

I looked around my little home and noticed more glass. The windows, obviously; drinking ware, some red vases on a table, a few more pieces that belonged to my Scandinavian grand-mothers. On the desk sits a picture frame, a montage of shots taken at a friend's wedding, a day of much-needed laughter. In the drawer lies another frame—the glass broken where it hit the wall. The picture of someone in uniform scratched by the breaking glass and then smoothed; as if by salvaging one could mend that which ended in words as shattering as a bullet.

All around me are the colors of glass—red and green, crystal pieces picking up the sun that shines so brightly this day, making me smile. A dark piece that reminds me of the obsidian that is used for surgical instruments. Healing pieces to be held by cool hands in the dark. In a bowl is a small rosary, waiting in faith.

In a drawer, a small glass angel grasped tightly in my hand one long day and night, many years ago. In my mind there is still a reflection of a small form in that little angel, tiny white fingers still smelling of the womb, soft reddish hair, her form placed on my stomach for only a moment. I had been afraid to touch her, the palm of my hand bloody from holding that angel so tight those many hours of travail that I'd flayed it open, the doctor unaware it was even with me. I saw my daughter's form in the glass; she saw her future in my eyes; and we both formed words neither of us were capable of articulating.

In the kitchen sits a small glass bowl, stained and scarred from the merry-go-round of water spray that was the top shelf of the dishwasher at my parents' house. I didn't need another bowl, but when Dad was cleaning out stuff and asked, "Do you want anything from this old kitchen stuff?" I had to bring it home with me in my suitcase.

When I was a child I had a goldfish named General Finn, one in a long line of goldfish who happily swam and then went to their final rest with a wave of the Ty-D-Bol man and a couple of solemn words. Not wishing to spend the money on a formal tank, Mom cleaned out the bowl without fail every week until I was big enough to handle the glass myself. During the cleaning, she would carefully scoop General Finn up in her hand and place him gently in the little green bowl where he waited in fresh water until his big bowl was clean. Now it just sits empty—but when I see it, scuffed and clouded, I remember my mom and those little things that she used to do, thinking I'd never ever remember.

I wonder if my daughter ever thinks of the one thing I did for her—bigger than anything, yet such a simple act, as small and clear as a falling tear.

She's turning eighteen this year. I wonder if she's going to call me?

On the wall empty vessels suspended in air, sharp against a background of light, containing nothing, but containing everything. Light and form and dark and shadow collected and radiated into the room. When I was studying martial arts my Zen Master said, "Emptiness is form and form is emptiness"— and looking at the glass I finally grasp what he meant. One minute the glass is nothing but a vessel, the next it is the vessel for all that surrounds it.

Glass. Objects formed of science and whim; shaped and molded to possess and display, to cut or heal; lasting for a century if cared for and broken beyond repair with the slightest of doubts. Glass objects hold, they feed, they nurture, and they lay things wide open with sharpness and light.

So many things around us are as old as time and as necessary. Remembered there on what was a very long day, surrounded by empty vessels, fragmented and silent, and awaiting my tending. As I worked away I heard the intake of my breath, in and out, fueling the beat of my heart, the whoosh of blood in my veins. Form is emptiness and emptiness is form. As I did what needed to be done, my mind opened; my body filled with purpose and need, as strong as obsidian but fragile as glass.

Home now, I sit and look at the fading light seeking shelter within. In the window the flash of a fin, swirls and shapes of light, form, and movement that glint on my skin, kissing it with lips as cool as glass. On the desk a goblet in which frozen water lay in a pool of amber—the Irish whiskey, a taste of a sharp knife, not cutting.

The sun drops below the horizon. The old vase falls into darkness, the fish still there, yet not, their spirits long since lifted up to sanctuary and refuge. In my hands lie glass beads, lying there like bullets as I recite a litany of prayer for those empty forms.

29

Surviving the Battle

Battles have been fought in the air from the first day a small dove dived down from the talons of a hawk. Man was not far behind.

Watching a movie about the dogfights of World War I, I realized the battle was not much different than any sporting event played on a field, the field being simply three-dimensional. The pilots would swing and soar and dive, maneuvering their craft with the unmistakable prodigal swagger that is their testament, over shattered roads and islands of tilled earth, desolate above the destruction which they carried.

A man's death was much less about firepower than simply the consequence of being bettered in a fair contest with someone much like himself. Those who survived held court not as enemies but as gentlemen heroes, remembering those dogfights as the best of what were otherwise insensible and ceaseless battalions of time.

The few that came home did so to lives that were fixed by

gravity and obligation, growing thicker and quieter; raising a glass of amber liquid in the evening; finding that being dead while still breathing was a lot less peaceful than they expected. But most did not survive. Their legacy lay among the tumbled ruins of war; the movement of lips as names were read; a photograph of a pretty girl that had already begun to fade.

I look at a picture in my wallet—so worn from touch as to be as fragile as ancient paper.

My dad was part of the 8th Air Force barely out of his teens. Though not a pilot, he came home with pictures and stories of those years there—metaphors of daring, chronicles of speed that to my mind would always have the indisputable stamp of the heroic on them. My uncles as well were in the Air Force. One of them, Uncle Rich, came back to be an engineer for Boeing, his office filled with drawings that to us were as mythical as dragons, esoteric shining shapes from which fire roared as the heavens shook.

It was not unexpected then that I came home one day as a teen and said, "I'm going to learn how to fly," which was met with about the same level of support as, "I'm going to shave my head and join a cult." I can't blame Dad; with redheaded children he had seen his share of wild ideas—most of which we abandoned before we actually blew anything up.

The fact that I only had a minimum wage job slinging submarine sandwiches didn't deter me. I got a job at the local airport pumping gas and washing aircraft for minimum wage and was able to get my lessons at a discount, sometimes trading a wash or wax for a couple hours of instruction from the owner who was a certified flight instructor. Dad said, thinking he was out of earshot: "She won't last the week." After the first couple of days of driving around that big fuel truck, hauling hose and climbing ladders out in the bitter cold, I was likely to agree with him, but for wanting to prove him wrong. For such are challenges both external and internal, hot and cold, fatigue and muscle pain; the miscalculations that can cost you not just your job but your life.

Still, the old tailwheel airplane I learned in paled against the aircraft of those old stories, bearing in my adventuresome mind all the excitement of a draft horse. So I'd go to air shows, finger tracing the outline of a cowl, taking in the scent of kerosene that bears with it some primordial fragrance of dinosaurs fighting to the death. I'd not touch that which wasn't mine; I'd ask questions, and I'd simply sit and listen to those stories that fueled my dream. When a couple of biplanes showed up to live on the field where I worked, the fascination grew even as some around me said, "You're a girl, you'll never make it in that profession," or, "You're going to just get yourself killed."

But I did not think of such craft by any means as being a threat to me when operated with logic and calm, any more than I think I'm limited by what I can do based on the plumbing God gave me or anything other than my mind. Rather it's the measure of that which I have proven I can do, of what I can achieve. Some of those early airplanes might have been small, but what they brought to me can't be destroyed.

Earthbound we have limitations as varied as our lives. As pilots, life is simpler. Our will is freer; our lives, however different, are truer and more defined. No matter what we cherish in life, we cherish it more: home, friends, and the smell of freshly tilled earth from a mile up; the heady gulp of pristine, crisp air that clears both our lungs and our heads.

Like anyone for whom life involves the complexity of hand and will, even when we pilots aren't flying we tend to hover around the airport, drawn like moths to a flame. We show up to have a cup of coffee and grasp the collective knowledge of those that have gone before us; taking in the stories, the tall tales, the wisdom. The knowledge that is passed on from veteran to youngster and from instructor to student is like a flame—the warmth of recognition of what we recognize in each other, the pulse of blood within the hand that reaches out and offers to share the knowledge and wonder.

Many a day was spent whiling away an hour on little excursions of self-discovery, edged with moments of "&*#*! You've got it." With the help of a good instructor I learned not just colorful language, but the patience to sense the mood of the wind before it knocked on my windshield, the curve of a farm field, and the lay of a grass runway.

There's something about learning to fly in an old tailwheel airplane. You'll freeze in her, you'll sweat like a sumo wrestler in her, dodge seagulls, balloons, and summer rain clouds in her. There's no glass, no electronic warning systems, no autopilot; simply a pure by-the-seat-of-your-pants adventure that hearkens back to simpler times in faraway farm fields. There's the wind in your hair, the sound of insects whirring in the fields; and then a quiet night with a glass of amber liquid, not as mourning for what is lost but as communion with what remains.

But it was time to move on; a slot far away to go learn how to fly the big and the bulky, to take up the mantle of doing something with my life that was beyond the safety of a small town—a history without effort. I wasn't sure how I would do with a life of structure, rules, and "I have to dress like everyone else?" But it was time to grow up and look at the horizon as more than my playground.

Before I left to don that uniform, I took one more flight in my old tailwheel airplane. In that moment I could pretend to be a fighter pilot, dodging sunbeams and sparrows out high above a farmer's field, smiling at the feel of the plane's power and the response to my controls. The craft for this one perfect moment in time an extension of both my hands and my will. As I pulled the control stick back, the sun hit my eyes, a flash, a glare—this moment not the steady flame of everyday existence but that one bright flash of a struck match that burns so much stronger than valor or fear, if only for this moment.

Now, sixteen years later I was taking another such flight, this time not in goodbye but in anticipation. It was my daughter's eighteenth birthday, the day she would be provided my contact information from the agency that handled the adoption.

Life was coming around full circle, my days of flying behind me but for an occasional flight for fun, a new career begun; and perhaps, just perhaps, a chance to bond with the one person for whom time had been held suspended for eighteen years.

As the wheels chirped upon the pavement in that final landing, shadows bowed before a wavering sun, the chill in the air an intractable summons of fall here in early summer skies. This was going to be my last such flight for a while as flying for fun is a lot more expensive than flying for a living. I pulled my leather bomber jacket around me, not because I was chilled but to draw in a deep breath, to sustain me in the airless days ahead.

As I left that little hangar, I looked at the photos on the wall of old pilots and old war birds from generations ago. Even as those men stood there silently, they radiated their destiny, leaning against those winged forms of man's imagination, looking not into the camera, but somewhere beyond—at some small piece of heaven, glimpsed for just a moment as the sun breaks through the clouds, then disappearing forever with the clap of thunder.

I give a quiet little salute and shut the hangar door to darkness.

30

Full Circle

There is an imperceptible pause of a life in the moment between the event and the moment of the knowing. After it's happened, but when it hasn't yet been formed into words. The click between one life and another. The phone rings early and I'm sleeping so soundly I think it's in my dream. It's for me and it's a hesitant: "Hello... Is that you?"

My daughter had called—not on her eighteenth birthday but only a few weeks later, after she'd had time to think about it. She thought I'd be much older than I was, wondering why I didn't keep her as only a single working woman. She didn't know I had been practically a child myself, not even able to put food on the table without occasional help from my dad. I'm not sure where she got that idea as news about me to her parents was minimal, but I'm glad the information provided to her on her birthday cleared up her questions even as I now had a million of my own.

I was thrilled to find out that not only was she happy and healthy, she'd had an idyllic childhood like mine, one of play and imagination and two parents to loved and supported her. As I had expected, her parents had given her their own name. Her name was Rebecca, a lovely name from the Bible.

In talking, for hours, for days, we discovered that we are alike in so many ways. Rebecca is a mirror image of me, but with her parents' heart and laughter. We love steak, macaroni and cheese, and reading. We both loved the movie *The Princess Bride,* and she loved the outdoors, which I breathed in deeply.

We had the same haircut; we owned almost all of the same books. We laughed to find out her boyfriend's name was Justin, the name I was going to give her if she was a boy. They were serious, and it would not be long after their college graduation that Justin would not be my son, but my son-in-law.

As we went through the process of becoming friends with each other and I heard in detail the wonder of those happy, secure early years growing up, I was amazed at my role in this. When I met her mom for the first time, a beautiful Hawaiian woman, she grabbed me in a big bear hug, openly crying and thanking me for my gift of "our daughter." Moments like that make life real.

When Rebecca graduated from university not long thereafter, a National Merit Scholarship winner, I watched quietly from the crowd as an invited guest, with as much pride as any parent there. I didn't let her know I was there, not wishing to take something from her day with her friends paying more attention to "Look, it's her biological mom!" than "Look, we graduated!"

But I was so happy to see it, even at a distance. I treasure my family, and her family is as dear to me as my own. But when holidays roll around, my joy is occasionally bittersweet and the reality of what I had to give up stirs in my heart. The mother-daughter bonding, Girl Scouts, camping, that first prom, all of which I only experienced in my heart's longing. But she is in my life now with her parent's blessing. That is what my life is now, small precious moments, sharing with someone so like myself, yet living her own dreams.

Some people may say I didn't do the right thing. But I did. For my precious child I did the absolute best I could. It is not society's or the media's role to judge my decision to give her up; that is something that only I can do as I look in the mirror each morning. And it certainly is not a reflection on the kind of person I was at eighteen or what kind of parents I had. We make our choices, we make good and bad decisions; and if we have any strength of character, we own up to them and try to make them right.

31

Flight Plans

In aviation, pilots often file what is known as a "fight plan." A flight plan is the route one is going to fly and at what altitude, how much fuel you have, how many people are on board, expected time of arrival (so someone can look for you if you are late), etc.

One item that goes on the flight plan if the weather is forecast to absolute crud (that's a precise meteorological term you usually don't hear on the weather channel) is an alternate airport. Because in flying, like anything in life, things often don't go as planned.

It was going to be one of those days. I was supposed to fly out and visit my daughter Rebecca and her husband, when a winter storm closed down her airport. I had the time off and the tickets, but now I was stuck at home on my days off. The weather out in the Rockies was fickle, the late spring wedding they had earlier in the year starting with ten inches of snow.

If you really think about it, most things go that way.

How many times have you planned a flight, a vacation, or a night out, and someone gets sick, the weather turns bad, or you made the mistake of using a cut-rate travel site and your luxury beach romp for $199 per person turned into the *Alabama Chain Gang Holiday*? How many times did you get that cranky crew chief that didn't like either pilots *or* prolonged eye contact? (If you do, don't blink, don't ever blink.)

How many times did life sometimes mark you, pulling away bits of flesh or even a heart without a suture to mark it closed so it will heal, nothing left but the fading whisper of guns and the descending of flags?

Some folks can't handle change, expecting that life will go a certain way, and by God, it had better—and they don't really do well when it doesn't. I was in a CVS and witnessed a guy chew out the clerk as he bought his four pizzas, three boxes of cigarettes, and half gallon of Tequila with an almost hysterical "By God, you don't have any more of the breakfast sandwiches with sausage, and what the hell am I going to eat?!"

My dad is not that type, instead letting things roll off of him like water—perhaps why he survived adopting and raising two redheads when he was already middle-aged.

Dad has always been active in the community and the church, as well as his local Chapter of the Lions Club. One thing he was particularly proud of was the Chapter's newspaper recycling fund-raising program. It provided income for community and scholarship programs—but not without a lot of hard volunteer work. The shining marker of that program was a newspaper recycling facility built to further expand on that community project. The members constructed it themselves: husbands and fathers, grandfathers and great-grandfathers, laboring in cold and rain, heat and sun, often at the expense of their own sleep. In November 2000, newly constructed, vandals burned it to the ground.

There was nothing left but a few support timbers, lined up in stark order like gravestones at a military service. The men, Dad included, simply stood there stunned as water dripped from the remains, strips of clouds like bayonets against the sky. A lot of work went into the recycling center, all done by volunteers and many of them World War II vets in their seventies. You would have expected my dad to storm and rage against a senseless act of destruction. But he didn't, though I was not so naive that I didn't miss the simmering outrage within which lives a betrayal too intense and inert to ever be articulated.

On the flip side, I remember Mom's funeral. I was pretty young, not a child but still wet behind the ears, and I was trying to help Dad as much as I could. He realized before the service that he needed a haircut, his not having paid any attention to that sort of thing the last few months of her life. I offered to help. I got out the clippers, turned them on and made my first path through his hair (though bald on top, he had some fine red hair on the sides). Uh-oh. Apparently you're supposed to put a *guard* on there to get it the right length. I'd shaved him clear down to the scalp.

Other than shaving his favorite football team's name on his head, there was nothing to do but shave it all. He went to Mom's service looking like Mr. Clean. No one dared say anything. But you know, Dad hugged me, made some great jokes about it, and held his head up high as he said goodbye to his first great love.

It made it easier a few years later when, in support of a girl-friend diagnosed with breast cancer, a couple of us shaved our heads in support. Only she ended up with a lumpectomy and just radiation, kept her hair, and we looked like Goth biker chicks for several months.

But I was OK, because I learned from Dad that whatever bad things may happen to us, there is only one thing that allows them to permanently damage our core self—and that is continued belief in them. You may cry, you may make that sound that is simple agony; but it is not the sound of relinquishment or acceptance, even if to the ear they are the same.

It's your choice. You can go through your days with intractable and unceasing conviction of the inherent instinctive duplicity of all men, including yourself. Or you can give folks around you the benefit of the doubt until they prove otherwise. That doesn't mean you assume man is never evil, for indeed he can be; and you may find that out in a moment that's like the false dawn between dark and light, when only God's winged and four-legged creatures know and sound the alarm which you may not hear. For those moments you are prepared.

But in your day-to-day activities with friends, colleagues, and neighbors, practice patience and trust. When things don't go as planned or someone does something with the best of intentions you'd rather they didn't, simply smile and help them fix it—or ignore it and move on. When someone betrays you, forgive (but never forget the bastard's name).

It's simply a matter of perspective. When you have a fight, a failure, or a Charlie Foxtrot on our hands—as you may when human will, machinery, or Mother Nature are involved—you can shake your fist and cry your tears until you drown in them. Or you can dry your eyes, pick up the pieces, and make something of value with what's left. You may even find that what you thought you wanted was not what you needed, finding a happiness you never expected by the loss of what you did. For what some people think will make them happy—no challenges, no bends in the road, only expected behaviors and outcomes—is for others something else. For those such people, the predicable and easy is but an old, flat habituation for which no effort is made to move beyond it; until they are so used to that life that they fail to smell and taste it.

My day did not go as planned; my weekend did not go as planned; the chance to travel to see my child now gone. I could simply say that I shoveled a boatload of snow and slept alone. And that would be true, but it is not—because my time was what I made of it, not what was taken from it.

It was warm sheets going on smooth and taut with the remembered motion of hands. It was pastry formed and rolled and layered with fresh butter and remembered motion. It was play-time with a puppy. It was time to remember, to say thanks as I looked down upon the creeping ridge of snow and ice before my shovel. *Not* with anger but with astonishment for the divine snowy brightness that for just this moment forgave an imperfect landscape its transgressions.

It was one phone call that made me look at the whole world a bit differently. Because for the first time since Allen and I had bonded as children, on this day when I heard a voice that sounded exactly like mine, I felt like I belonged.

There would be other phone calls from Rebecca, plans to meet sometime in the coming year. Outside the birds twittered with happiness, having found the bird seed strewn out across the dry, clear ground. The snow had ended, the light growing bright, graduating from gray to rose to the sky's ultimate sapphire. I wrapped a warm blanket of gold about me, looking out onto the mist of frozen water as I savored the myriad waking sounds of life.

32

The Rescuers

Life was good. I talked to my brother as often as I always had. Now I got to talk to my daughter as well. I had a black Lab and a new house, the world brimming with possibility.

When the phone range late one night, I recognized the voice. The caller was in law enforcement, a female friend, not a colleague. We chitchatted regularly; but a call this late was not good news and I was afraid it was professional in nature. She said, "I need you to help me rescue a dog."

Apparently, the deadbeats who'd been living in an old rental house down the road from her place booked out in the middle of the night. She saw the vehicles loading up and leaving. Good riddance, she thought. Then, late at night, carried on the wind she heard the pitiful cry.

A coyote? A dog? The neighbors are gone, it must be someone else, she thought. The next night she didn't hear it over the cold wind, but on the third night she did, a high pitched whine of a soul's abandonment. The house remained dark; the utter stillness, complete silence a testament to the tears outside.

My friend crept over, seeing no sign that the residents were anything but gone; the house empty of belongings, the yard covered in trash. It was a pup, a retriever, purebred from its looks, left chained up in the backyard with a bowl of rain water and no food. Left to die when they vacated in a hurry. She called: "I need backup." I knew what she meant. So off I headed, taking no purse, only the gear in my truck, some cash, and dog treats in my pocket. When I got there the house was definitely vacant; no meth heads would be coming back and surprising us.

As we approached, even in the dark we could see that the poor animal, a young dog, was starving and cold. The temperatures had been reaching down in the forties. Tonight was gray and even colder, with a forecast of freezing rain. For now the sky held in the moisture, refusing to release it; but it was supposed to go below freezing soon. The dog wouldn't have survived the night, its only companion the smell of water and blood.

Blood? Why did I smell blood?

My friend, crouched down over the dog as I stood watch, pointed at something. Hard-nosed law officer though she was, she had tears in her eyes: the dog had outgrown her collar, and it was actually was cutting deep into the flesh, leaving bloody tracks in what should have been the soft fur of contentment. The poor animal had to be in terrible pain, but she only licked our hands and tried to snuggle up. My friend asked, "Can you get it out?" I always have some first aid and medical type implements in my bag, but I had to say, "I've never cut on anything still breathing." I expected the dog to bite me as I worked gently with small tools to free it. But she just continued to nuzzle our hands, even though in my attempt to remove this tiny round torture device I had to be causing her more pain.

I looked up to the sky, thinking for a moment the clouds had finally given up their rain, when I realized that what was on my tongue was the taste of salt as I worked away.

When finally we stood up, the dog in my friend's arms and the remnants of that collar lying on the ground like a broken mirror, we heard the crunch of tires. Both of us were poised for fight or flight until we saw that it was local law enforcement. There was the flash of red and blue, of a bright flashlight, the glint of a shield. We smiled, hands in view, thankful for assistance and my friend was recognized with a "What are you ladies doing out here?!" My friend called out, "Hey D.!" He replied, calling her by name, ". . . .What *are* you doing out here? I was keeping an eye on this place in case they were back and up to no good."

She said, "I'm just stealing this dog, sir." He looked at the dog, a puppy really, then looked at me and said, "Who's this?" She told him who I was, his eyes smiled as he recognized the name, and he chuckled and said, "And what are *you* doing out here?" I said. "*Helping* her to steal this dog, *sir!*"

He just laughed. Calling the local animal officer was suggested, but we told him, given this very remote and rural area, that might take an hour or more; the pup was in bad shape and had lost blood, she could die if we didn't do something. My friend told the officer we'd take the dog to the vet, pay the bill ourselves, and get her a good home. The dog clearly was a stray in the eyes of the law, abandoned to die. The officer just said, "Dog? What dog? I didn't see any dog," and tucked some money in our hands to help toward the vet bill before he helped us load up and drove off.

The dog was cleaned up at the vet's office, an after-hours emergency call. The wound would not cause any permanent damage but was serious. In a few hours that gentle little retriever was bandaged up and home at my friend's. After we raised an amber toast in crystal goblets, recognition among tired friends, the pup curled up to sleep near the fire, joining a household that already had two spoiled, well-loved dogs.

As I looked at their forms and my own, I realized that life brings us friends in many forms—both two- and four-legged, both with their own healing power of Grace.

33

Anchors

The Little Prince lived alone on a tiny planet no
larger than a house . . .

—Antoine de Saint-Exup*éry*

The suitcase looked empty but it was not. There on the bottom
lay a small, carefully folded piece of paper with some writing
on it. I read it and I smiled.

The bag's opened up, some toiletries spread around the hotel
bathroom. Another day on the road. I guess the wandering
spirit runs in my blood, passed on from my Air Force father to
me. Seems like ever since I got a control yoke in my hand, I've
been wandering across miles of land, across rivers and towns in
whatever way I can, be it dromedary-like transport plane, rag-
gedy land rover, or swayback mule.

I always have an anchor. Over time it's been a small house, a
large house; it's also simply been a suitcase and the friends who
love me. But when I'm there I am thoroughly happy; for that
anchor instead of being a confinement is simply the base from

which I move, a fulcrum that amplifies the effects of my motion, the beat of my heart.

Saint-Exupéry wrote, "He who would travel happily must travel light." And so I did, the earliest memories little more than the remembered feel of the starched uniform shirt I wore, the dense oily smell of jet fuel lingering on the tongue like smoke. It seems as if all my early years were reflected in the windows of those moving airplanes. I see my reflection, my past, through bug-splayed glass that tinted the world bright.

The airplane, the destination, and the years changed as did the landscape of my career, but some things never do. Days in an airplane traveling far. Miles and hours spent watching the landscape, silver grain elevators, red-winged birds, mountains formed of ice and fluid need, and rivers without borders. All blending into a bright diorama of life racing past. The world looks different from above, clouds massive and dark looming up like a target in a gun sight, looking twice the size of ordinary man.

It seems I have spent a half of my life on my way to nowhere. I have watched a hundred cumulus clouds erupt, the mass assassination of flying insects, and the disappearance of a slice of apple pie at a tiny airport diner; and the journey was only beginning.

With each day comes another opportunity for adventure. This particular day, the ride to the hotel alone was something to remember. A shuttle service, stopping at several hotels on the way; the sullen driver demonstrating why driving was his second language. You know how when most people drive, certainly professional drivers, they brake using an increase in pressure on the brake pedal so as to come to a smooth stop? Not Mr. Shuttle. The only brake technique he used was to stomp on the brake, let up, let the car roll, stomp again. It would take four or five of these stomps to equal one normal braking action. No traffic, heavy traffic, it made no difference.

I started to feel like a bubblehead doll, and saving 25 dollars over a taxi was beginning to look like one of those small decisions that had great, over-sized repercussions. But perhaps I should have been more patient: I guess it was hard to concentrate on braking when one is texting while driving in heavy traffic.

I simply made sure my seat belt was fastened and then bent down as if into a stiff wind, horns of the impatient exploding into the rain-split asphalt that opened and closed with opportunity. Like all traffic in big cities, we carried on—sharp with speed and then trickling to a standstill; the road dipping into the fog like a hand cleaving water; the headlights showing the gray bulk of streams of cars coming down the hill like rain.

When the last guest got off and it was just me, the driver quit texting and had a series of increasingly heated exchanges in his mother tongue with his dispatcher about how he only got 47 US dollars in fares for this trip, and he wanted to get a number one spot when he got back to the airport. (Actually, sir, you got 68 dollars in fares, one that you did not log and pocketed instead. I notice things like that). The arguing got more heated. I am not fluent in a ton of languages. I can simply listen and relate small things in a number of languages that come in handy, Russian, Chinese, French, just enough to know when it's a good time to get out of Dodge or when happy hour is almost over. It comes in handy, the knowing, the looking, I thought as I caught quick glimpses of other drivers in the failing sunlight, faces fixed and grim as they fought to get upstream.

The van driver, still yelling into the phone while almost whacking several people on bicycles, finally stopped in front of my hotel. I paid him the fare plus a ten percent tip. He did *not* look happy, expecting much more from the American redhead in nice clothes.

He muttered something under his breath about what he had to do to get a big tip, and I replied:

«Вам надо научиться использовать торможения.»

(Translation: "You need to learn how to use the brakes.")

He was still standing there, mouth agape, when I went up to my suite.

But I had arrived. The hotel bulked long and dark against the city sky, but inside was golden warmth, a bite of fresh apple, a much needed bottle of water. Sitting still for a minute took care of the aching neck; and soon it was time to meet a colleague for dinner while we went over notes for tomorrow's activities.

After a short walk back to the hotel, my colleague making sure I got to my room safely, I made a couple phone calls to loved ones, wanting to let them know I was in and safe. My dad always worries when I travel, even when I don't tell him where I'm going; so do friends; and I try and keep in touch. Then I took a long bath in a tub so deep you could hide a mastodon in it and slept until 6:30 in the morning. Unfortunately it was 6:30 in the morning where I *wanted* to be, not where I *was*.

So I got up and made coffee and watched a stain of light snare itself between steel and rain, spreading until the stain grew light and the light became morning.

By choice or not, travel is still part of my life. But travel brings something to you that people who live in the insular world of their home town their whole lives may miss: it pushes your boundaries. When you travel you can become invisible, if that is what you choose. I like that. I like to be the quiet observer as I walk among the walls of a quiet place of history. What stories would that old building tell, what makes these people who they are—what heartaches do they carry within their own baggage?

You may have work that takes much of your time; yet still in this strange place there are hours open to you. You don't have a lawn to mow or bills to pay. There is only life, as simple and inescapable as an empty hallway, where for a moment you can leave behind the burdens that you freely assume and carry as brightly and ambitiously as brass. For this moment you are simply a creature of discovery, free to visit stately buildings, savor a cup of coffee, or simply go watch the trains.

The suitcase is open in a simple wooden stand. It is empty, but there is so much in it. The smell of crushed sage from a bounce across the desert in a jeep; the wood-burnt smokes of a small cabin; the smell that is long-untouched ground after a rain; the rich earth scent of something being warmed that had for so long been cold. The crisp, fragile pieces of an old and carefully folded letter—the first I ever received from Rebecca.

34

The Note

The note from my daughter was sent not long after we met for the first time, written on paper she likely had from her school work, carefully folded and tucked into an envelope.

The poem is one that I had not read before; I later found it on a number of adoption websites, listed as author unknown.

But there, written in my child's delicate feminine hand, the words moved me to tears.

"Once there were two women who never knew each other.

One - you do not remember, the other you call mother.

Two different lives shaped to make yours,

One became your guiding star, the other became your sun.

The first gave you life, and the second taught you to live in it.

The first gave you a need for love and the second was there to give it.

One gave you a nationality; the other gave you a name.

One gave you the seed of talent; the other gave you an aim.

One gave you emotions; the other calmed your fears.

One saw your first sweet smile; the other dried your tears.

One gave you up - that's all she could do.

The other prayed for a child and God led her straight to you.

Now you ask through all your tears the age-old question
through the years;

Heredity or environment - which are you a product of?

Neither, my darling - neither - just two different kinds of love."

The apple doesn't fall far from the tree. I'm not sure where the phrase came from, but looking at our children, those we love, it stands to reason. When we hold them for the first time we move with such caution, speaking in hushed tones, recognizing something within us that had always slumbered, slightly alive, just waiting to be born.

After she was born I moved from the state, finding it easier to keep my promise to not contact her from a distance. I'd like to say the span of years passed quickly, but the reality was more protracted. There's a line in Shakespeare's *Othello* that says, "There are many events in the womb of time that will be delivered." Womb of time? Yes. The sweat of endurance, the agony of spreading bone. Nothing worthwhile is easy or quick, but oh, at the end it is worth the travail of time.

When we did meet, several things struck me, especially in that I had not seen her since birth. Rebecca looked exactly like me.

Not just the face, the coloring, the unusual almond shaped eyes. We also wore clothing almost identical in form and style. We ordered the same item on the menu, had the same habits, the same mannerisms, the same laugh. Yet she is who she is, the loving heart, the talent, the drive, from the two wonderful people who raised my child, their daughter, one Hawaiian, one Irish American.

Genes or environment? Who's to say? It's both, it's neither, and it's something we can only watch in wonder. But whether they are like us or simply their own persons, we see something in them. We see a journey: ours—and theirs. We're the rim and they're the spokes, spreading out, seeking ground, moving away, yet always close to us. We're both part of a journey that is worth every bit of the wear, every mile.

Such thoughts came to me when I was out in the field during that quiet questing about the scene, gathering, watching. It's hard because sometimes children are involved. But underneath my gear I felt the trace of a wallet in my back pocket, in it as always that well-worn tear-stained photo of a beautiful fair-haired girl with blue eyes.

It's why I do what I do. Its why when we look in to the trusting eyes of a child we see not ourselves but the foretaste of responsibility, the fierce need to keep them safe no matter what.

And so it was I reflected on such things that last day out in the field, looking up at branches shattered by forces bigger than themselves, hanging in the air as if part of the earth was thrust upward, and a spectral tracing to a loss more profound than simply lost years.

Somewhere that night a family would grieve. Somewhere that night, through no effort of mine but a heart laid wide open, my child lay safe.

I looked up at broken trees to a heaven unbroken and simply said thanks.

35

On Being a Grown-Up

I was making more friends whom I cherished and had met more and more of Rebecca's extended family. Her mom and I have the same first name, so it was rather fun to see us both introduced. It was almost like that TV show with the two brothers named Daryl: "This is my mother L. and my other mother L." Adoption in the Hawaiian culture is as natural as breathing, and I was always made to feel a part of them—even as I kept enough distance most of the time so not to infringe on that bond my daughter would have with the one who was her true mother.

Between visits I had my friends, making more as the years went past; time soothing old hurts, the playful wag of a dog's tail bringing me out of my shell. Some of those friends were like family—the ones that will bail you out or hide that body, as it is said. If you're lucky they're not exactly like you, exposing you to new experiences, broadening your horizons. One of those is my friend Fred whom I have known for many years, though he lives several states away.

Several years ago I stopped in at a very large technology convention, while on annual leave to visit family in the local area. Fred was one of the speakers, and I wanted to go hear him talk and catch up on some of the technology. There were presenters from all over the world, civilian, military, government; and booths that would make any geek hyperventilate. After everyone gave their presentations we milled around with Fred's colleagues at the expo, perusing the super-cheap geek gadgets offered to everyone there and looking at the really cool stuff we couldn't take home. (Ooh! A Crypto Kids Coloring Book!)

The first night after the opening festivities there was an industry-hosted cocktail reception for a handful of VIPs (and some of their sidekicks), where beautiful women kept coming by with little bits of food. One such thing was what looked like plain beef on a stick. I figured I'd better taste one to be polite though I wasn't really hungry. At lunch we had left convention food behind to wander the city for something a little more interesting.

Still full from lunch, I intended to try only one, just to be sociable.

On my first taste all I could think of was: *What* manner of bovine divine *IS* this?

The tiny and drop-dead gorgeous Japanese server, who looked like she could either (1) charm anyone alive or (2) snap me like a twig, said with great pride: "It's Kobe Beef."

Kobe beef refers to cuts of beef from the black Tajima strain of Wagyu cattle raised to strict tradition in Hyōgo Prefecture, Japan. The meat is unbelievably expensive and prized as a delicacy, renowned for its flavor, tenderness, and well-marbled fatty texture. It is rumored that these cattle are fed beer and ice cream and massaged daily with sake. (Where do I sign up?) I'm not sure exactly how the cattle are raised, but it's not a cheap meat. There's a reason it tastes as it does, and true Kobe—not "Kobe style"—steaks can cost hundreds of dollars. As my food budget with student loans and a new home was more navy beans and cornbread, it would probably be a while (as in: when the sun implodes) before I would be able to have Kobe beef again.

Let's just say I had more than one. That woman and her tray orbited around me like I was my own planet (which I would have been if I'd eaten more), and every time she made the rounds I'd have to try one before they were all gone.

The next night there was cocktail reception in a big ballroom for some of the presenters and their guests, hosted and paid for by one of the private industry companies that were sponsoring the whole shindig. I wasn't there in any official capacity, just as Fred's buddy; but I was on the guest list and therefore expected. A former President was also a guest, so the security was ultra-tight. But I had the special pass and was in—though I had to leave my ninja toys behind in my hotel room. I also had to dress up, meet some folks to make polite conversation, and promise not to TP any current or former politicians.

Maybe I'm the only person who feels this way, but I usually feel like I'm just a little kid occupying a grown-up's body. I'm not a female James Bond, I'm not comfy in crowds and rarely get invited to fancy parties outside of work, and I don't want to. I'm comfy in my secret kid identity. The kid has no titles and isn't in any magazines or newspapers. I'm just L. B., Colonel H.'s little girl, baker of cookies, teller of bad jokes and science puns, owner of some cool toys, and I have some really amazing playmates. I cry at the playing of taps, Amazing Grace, and the funeral scene in *Star Trek II: The Wrath of Khan*. I can still cry when the mean girls are unkind to me. I can still kick the snot out of a lot of the boys. So normally at these sorts of events I feel out of place, though I do a good job of blending in with the scenery. It's a science. But it's not my natural element even if I can act like a grown-up when required to protect and defend.

Yet also in the same flesh is an adult. One who can pull on her boots and in the middle of the darkest of nights rise above slumber's respirations to tackle the undefended throat of the unwary, tools in hand.

But most of the time I just feel like a little kid. The baby photo in my wallet has been replaced by one of my daughter and her husband. I look at her and ask myself, "How can I have a child that age? I'm just a kid myself," our own eyes failing to note an aging process that usually doesn't include the mind.

So that night Fred was in a tux; some colleagues in attendance were engaged in tactical repartees as they commented on the guests. I was wandering around in full grown-up mode, on the list as Fred's guest, doing my best to not trip in my high heels; when something caught not my eye but my nose. But what was that wonderful aroma, it's familiar but. . .?

In addition to all sorts of fancy appetizers, they had not just Kobe Beef but *Kobe Beef Sliders* and a mashed potato bar—where homemade mashed potatoes were served in big wine glasses with a long spoon and everything you could imagine to put on them. Bacon, onions, roasted garlic, cheeses, sour cream, and truffle-y mushroom things. They spared no expense, but the Kobe beef on freshly baked buns still was the star, the smell alone standing out above the scent of expensive silk and perfume. But after a couple of Sliders, a sip of wine, and several glasses of water, I had to find a ladies room. Unfortunately it was outside the super-secret security, and my "pass" was in my handbag that one of keynote speakers was holding. Inside with my identification and cell phone. Damn.

They were *not* going to let me back in.

I said, "But I'm Dr. B. I'm on the list." No ID, no way, green eyes, cocktail dress notwithstanding. Look, I understand. It's their job whether I agree or not. Finally I gave the security fellow the full green eye wattage and said: "There's a clipboard there with my name and title on it, and it will show I initially checked in at 6:45. I have my ID at my table with the keynote speakers, you can see if you want to send someone in to get it. And to prove I just came from inside, I'm going to breathe on you. You'll understand."

He smiled and looked at me, puzzled at that last statement as he picked up the clipboard where, yes, my name was while someone went to fetch my ID. I gently leaned in towards him, a few inches from his lips and softly released my breath. He exclaimed: "*KOBE BEEF SLIDERS!!*"

I was *so* in.

Look, the world is full of fast food and easy decisions and safe adventures. You can walk the path most traveled, safely and with predictable tastes and textures and the acceptance of mainstream society. Or you can fuel up with Kobe beef or just some Chinese takeout and see where life takes you. Sometimes you get the stuffing knocked out of you, roads change course, or tools gets scuffed; yet you often find some things that are truly unique and wonderful along the way.

36
Water Reclaiming Our World

Life was good even as it rolled past too quickly. There were still those nights when I'd look to the West and wonder what my daughter was doing right now. But I knew she was happy, and that was the important thing.

I had an invitation to visit Rebecca soon as she was expecting a baby. But I first had a trip to make that would take me to one of the Great Lakes. I like sitting on the shores of those great bodies of water. Some winters Lake Eire freezes clear across, with great masses of ice that look like frozen waves piled up against the shores. Work has taken me there more than once; and when my day was done I would love to sit on one of the benches at water's edge. Bundled up against the chill, I would watch the earth slope to the water, the wind against my face a caress of cold, slow and pale.

I made one excursion there in the earliest days of spring, when winter was drawing to a close, shadows stirred, and the seasons shifted. Another winter away from the skies, those precious evenings aloft a memory brought in by the elements, herded inside like a recalcitrant horse to a dark barn. A winter's routine of chilled mornings and dark nights, cold absolution for the time I'd spent out in the sun in months past. I sat out on a bench by the water, no one around but a couple of solitary souls like me on other benches, each of us lost in thought. As I sat with the sound of breaking ice heralding the arrival of spring, I thought again of how quickly another season had flown away, time and tide waiting for no one. I thought of words I wish I'd been able to say to my daughter when we first talked on the phone, afraid I'd frighten her off if I told her I loved her; wondering if she would understand how you can love someone so much that you don't even know but for the visceral tug of a mother's heart.

"I remember my youth and the feeling that I will never come back anymore, the feeling that I could last forever, outlast the sea, the earth, and all men," Joseph Conrad wrote of his perilous adventures as a seaman on a storm-wracked coal liner. I know well that life, as a young woman seeking adventure that carried with it not just great duty, but great risk—never realizing at the time how close I'd come to the edge on occasion, sometimes simply for being in the wrong place at the wrong time.

That last night on Lake Erie I heard it in my cold breath as I sat seemingly frozen with a sense of imprecise hope, thinking back—to my youth. I realized that I too had ended up at the wrong place and the wrong time, but by making the right decision someone good came into the world to get the chance to make her own choices.

The lake seemed deceptively flat, as if you could walk on it. If you looked out beyond, you could see the motion as the ice was breaking up; and if you listened closely, you could almost hear a faint rumble as chunks of it broke, the movement of waves reclaiming their space disturbing the quiet. So much that rumbles underneath the surface of a seemingly calm life, heard only by some.

Even as kids spending summers on the Oregon coast, we weren't oblivious to the danger of the water, any more than I was unaware that the waters of this lake by which I sat that night were without risk. I'd been out enough in a small fishing boat to know that the waters, like the sky, hold their own dangers. Pilots of land or sky, we are always aware.

For you never know when things will turn bad. Even though now the sky is pure and the temperature is warm, the fact that spring is here is simply another sleight of hand from the greatest of magicians, Mother Nature. Winter never truly ceases, it only hides with the duplicitous strategies of an ancient enemy, old wounds only covered by the barest of springs before inflicting its grievance upon the earth again. It arrived to do battle when you least expected it, when the prolonged blow of the dark and ice sank through the skull and laid its claim deep on the bones of the winter landscape. In mere moments it could turn from the colorful quiet of new hope to a night not safe for man or beast.

There's always a risk. As much as I love to fly, I have spent enough hours aloft to know that the heavens are a two-edged blade, one of joy and one of violence that can cut you clean from the sky without a moment's hesitation. I thought about that now, alone and cold on the edge of a vast field of crashing ice as an osprey dove down for prey, his talons glinting in the last scrap of daylight.

As I sat out on the lake with only a couple of strangers watching the water with me from a distance, the rest of the community stayed home and warm, basking in the illusion that they were safe. Maybe illusion is really all they had. I'd rather be out here, facing the cold and the crashing ice, facing life. As a country on a warm September day a few short years ago, we learned the danger of what living with an illusion can do.

On this March day by Lake Erie, all of us here likely wondered the same things. What would life bring us in the coming year, bracing renewal or an end to our dreams? Would we be here this time next year to witness the ice break up? And if we were, would we even be the same people? The Greek philosopher Heraclitus wrote that you can't step into the same body of water twice. Maybe it was the same river twice, I couldn't recall the exact wording; but I did remember he said that just as the water ". . . is not the same, and is, so I am as I am not." Time and tide shape us; strengthening or eroding, we learn to stand hard and look at everything that approaches.

The high disinterested sky was darkening, and it was time to head back to my hotel; but I hesitated. Winter faded as darkness ascended. A great chunk of ice tore free as water reclaimed yet another area, sending seagulls into the air in alarm.

I wondered what this next year would bring me. A grandchild, of course; but hopefully a relationship with her as her mom's "other mother." I thought of the hours past, the torrent, the hours ahead, the hard and unyielding shore. I thought of the tragic mute bones that could have withstood anything that life threw their way if only left upright and undisturbed. Tears of joy splashed as water lapped onto rocks filling that void so secret and dark, waters that reclaimed our world.

37

Larry the Lion

The years passed, summer and fall, warm and wetness, in their immortal sequence. Rebecca was a mother now, having given birth to a daughter who was no more eager to come into the world than Rebecca herself had been. The first time I flew out to see the baby I was terrified I'd drop her, realizing that I had *zero* experience with infants. My daughter suffered my bumbling diaper changes with a patience I never had at her age and laughed with me late into the night with her husband as I heard more and more stories of those lost years.

After twenty years of being single I had happily remarried; someone much younger for whom I now knew a treasure trove of cougar jokes and a heart as full and round as the moon. He adored me, he adored my black Lab Barkley, and my family all loved him, especially my brother Allen who would spend hours in the kitchen at Dad's chatting engineer stuff with him. Watching them I felt little different than I did as a young woman but for the ache of "accu-knee"—my personal weather system that was installed when the Doc took care of a torn meniscus after a fall on ice. Getting old is not for wimps.

Looking around my tidy historic home that I now shared with my new husband, I noticed intricate wood lovingly restored; an old steamer trunk; artifacts from journeys around the world; the viscera of words, drawings, and maps; a blanket lying across the futon like a lover's shirt. On the walls pictures of railway trains, posters anatomizing mighty machines veined with steam and joints of steel.

Sitting there I realized how much I had gotten rid of over the last few years, those years spent with Barkley the Lab before I met my husband. Through selling or just giving them to friends in need, I had probably reduced my possessions by three quarters. What I had now would fit in a two-bedroom house, nothing bigger. I occasionally look at photos of the showpiece that was my previous home and feel a twinge of "Wow, that's beautiful." But I wasn't really happy there; it took all my time, all my money—and the only people who were dazzled by such luxury were the kind of people I didn't give a rip whether they were impressed or not.

Smaller was better, everything paid for but the roof over my head; the things I have left around me only the most meaningful possessions that speak of history, not ego. But looking at some wiring that was recently redone, I thought, what if the place caught fire some night or a flood was imminent, some sort of disaster? What would I take with me? It would be books, pictures, a soft blue shirt, badges of damage, and ribbons of courage.

Most things can be replaced: clothes, videos, a lot of the books, music, cookbooks. A lot of our photos today are on a hard drive backed up somewhere, not a photo album. But there are those things you can't replace, memories captured in small boxes, small heartbeats of time you can't get back. The small crafted things, made for you by others, or your dad's old uniforms. It's your life, and you only have a moment to grab those things that confirm you're alive, this archaeology of dreams.

First would be any living creature in the home, family, dog, or guest. If I had time, I'd grab the briefcase with the paper trail of my life, my pistol next to the bed, and whatever precious things are on the nightstand, my mom's picture, my badge, and my wallet. I'd also take, if I could, something that would make absolutely no sense to anyone but myself. I'd take a beat-up stuffed lion that stands guard.

Larry the Lion showed up one Christmas when I was about five. There were always wrapped presents under the tree, but Christmas morning there would also be something just from Santa that would be unwrapped and lying on the big brick bench around the fireplace. It was usually something *good* to go with the stocking loot. But it wasn't a lot. Dad explained later that he didn't think it right to get a ton of fancy toys from Santa and only one or two things from Mom and Dad, and then tell some kid at school who only got a shirt and new shoes from Santa and nothing else about all the toys he left for us. There are some things that aren't fair, but Dad said neither Santa nor Baby Jesus love unequally, only unconditionally.

Christmas mornings were always the same. We would wake

up Mom and Dad around 5:30 a.m., and they'd come dragging out to watch us look in wonder on what we'd been given,
shreds of wrapping paper scattered on the floor like spent brass.

I initially got the prerequisite baby doll stuff, but my parents
soon learned I was more of an "action toy"-type of girl. I later grew to love the trains, my Daisy rifle, and Legos; but one
plush toy sort of stole my little heart when I was so very young,
and he and I were inseparable for years.

It was Larry the Lion. I got him for Christmas one year when I
was running around on chubby legs, and I never let go of him.

Larry talked, and not the "goo goo gaa gaa" of most dolls. Larry
talked in Mel Blanc's voice. (Bugs Bunny, anyone?) When you
pulled his string he said about twelve different things: "I'm fe-
rocious, aren't I?" and "(*Growl*) OOOH! I scared myself!" and
"I'm a very, very, very brave Lion... Grrrr." When he spoke his
whole mouth moved, a soft plastic lion's mouth that responded
to both the pull of a string and the gentle kiss of a little girl.

Larry the Lion was my favorite stuffed companion for several
years. Then he was put aside as I discovered adventure that
lay outside my playroom, launching myself like rapture from
tree limbs, building models and trains, a carpenter of light and
noise. And that was fine by me, until I turned thirteen and
stuffed animals among young teenagers were suddenly cool.
But Larry was nowhere to be found.

I was certain Allen had taken him as a prank; holding him out in the playhouse or another secret fortress of play; waiting to trade him for something valuable. I also knew that wherever he was secreted, he was waiting for me. Listening with a quiet "I'm a very, very, very brave lion," as he stayed on a silent watch until I claimed him.

But he was just gone, never to be seen again. When I told Allen I thought he had taken Larry, he got that expression, sudden, intent, and concerned, that you just can't fake. My brother had a penchant for practical jokes, but he wouldn't hurt me for the world, and he helped me search. I missed Larry with that awareness of pages missing, longing with the unbridled hope of children even if I was much older. I tried to act like it was no big deal, being a cool teenager and all, bluffing my way into impending adulthood. But after combing the house for Larry I went into my room and cried, sound rupturing from someplace deep inside. I cried hard, perhaps because I had to cry quietly, perhaps because I felt the way about tears as I did about weakness: don't show it—but if you do, get it over and done with quickly, before anyone sees.

I looked one last time around the house a few years ago. Funny how some things just stay with you, but Larry was truly gone. After Mom died, Dad had gotten rid of so many of her things that were hard for him to see, touch, and feel. A putting away of memories that he believed were his to dispose of as he pleased. But these memories were still connected to Allen and me by tiny strands—filaments of touch and smell that would bring Mom back to us in those quiet moments when we'd sneak into a closet to touch what was gone. Things we needed, things no longer there. I don't blame Dad; he dealt with his grief in the way he could. But other than her badge from the sheriff's department, some cookie molds, and her housecoat, all Mom's clothes and personal things were given away, including most of the crafts and artwork she had done. Gone as if she'd painted a door and walked through it, never to return.

I figured Larry accidentally went out in that general removal of pain for my dad. As I entered adulthood and learned of loss of my own, I totally understood, even as I mourned with a lover's urge the dismantling of white picket fences and happy endings.

Then a couple years of ago I got a package from my home-town. While cleaning out a closet in the guest bedroom, Allen had found Larry—carefully packed by my mom in tissue and placed in a hatbox to be found after she passed. Allen got him boxed up and sent to me.

Larry arrived, carefully carried by the UPS man. I opened the box on an afternoon as quiet as the closet he had been hidden in; gently unfolding Larry from the tissue paper—still missing a whisker. He was a little dusty, needing a comb for his mane, and smelling of the sleep of reason that is childhood. When I pulled him carefully from the box he looked at me intently as if waiting for me to speak, if only in my imagination.

Surprisingly he could still talk as clearly as he did years ago; and I pulled his string again and again, laughing like a child.

In the rush of life and all it brings, Larry was sometimes ignored.

But like all true things he was always there, waiting quietly in the wings until I was ready. Until one night. I'd come in from a day out in the field. One of those days that followed me home, leaving invisible footprints from the door to my bed where I would walk in circles all night in my sleep, looking for that one thing I might have missed. Such days were hard; having to be tough, having to be impersonal; not knowing who is watching or if the media is nearby; brain deeply engaged, but heart floating spectral above the immense yet demarcated ruin filled with the voice of fire and grieving water.

I could call my husband but he would be asleep on the other side of the globe, away on a business trip. So I called my brother. I didn't tell him the details of the day, just as he didn't share the details of his, some things kept silent by choice or by honor. But I talked until I couldn't talk any more, simply telling Allen I missed him, sharing those stories of childhood.

As I walked through the house before bed, I saw Larry's shadow on the wall, the well-rubbed ears, the little ring on the string— and I pulled him close to me. I'd spent the day being tough, watching fate arrange the remains of what was left like a still life. I'd spent longer than that proving that such things don't leave on me the bruises of stories unfinished, that I don't get too attached to anything or anyone. But I do, with a capacity that has surprised me greatly, finding out emotion is not a measurable container.

I stood there, tired and dirty with a knee that felt like it was made of gunpowder, barbed wire, and scorpions. I could only stand, a grown woman, breathing deep the small form of a well-loved stuffed toy with a ratty mane and a missing whisker. There were no words for time when holding something that was precious, however untranslatable. Holding on tight, because he was all I could hold on to in that moment, sticking my face down into his fur, and for that instant being small and strong at the same moment.

I looked out onto a night that resisted words and to a photo of my brother by the bed. With a small smile I gave the string another quick pull as I held him close, if only to remind ourselves that we were both still very, very brave.

38

Roads Traveled

It was the end of my work week. I still lived in one city with my husband but worked in another large city a few hours away; so each week I had a bit of a drive. It was only for a year or two and I didn't mind the drive. The truck was running smoothly, I had water and supplies on board, one travel mug with coffee, one with Scooby Snacks. No GPS. I drive the truck simply with road sign navigation, finding the GPS voice a nagging I don't want and the directions sometimes less than accurate. (Recalculate this!) Certainly I get off course once in a great while, but sometimes those are the adventures we remember.

I was in South Florida on a layover with a copilot some years back. We'd heard there was a boat show, so we headed out in an old borrowed airport car to find it. What we found were miles and miles of small neighborhoods in which *no one* spoke English and boats were somewhat scarce. My Spanish is limited, just enough to get myself more thoroughly lost. I finally told my partner that the next business I saw, I *would* be stopping for directions, no matter what.

There, on the next corner was a small used car lot. But not just any used cars: they had all, for lack of a more politically correct term, been "pimped out." Lowriders, enough pink and glitter and chrome to take out an eye quicker than a laser. I couldn't imagine anyone over the age of twenty-two driving one of these in daylight with a straight face. The name of the place? *Get Down Motors.*

I said I was stopping, and I did, garnering a little attention as I did so, there not being a plethora of natural redheads around. The sales manager couldn't have been nicer, drawing me a map to where I was going, chatting for a bit about a couple of classic cars that in their prior lives might have inhabited the garage of our parents (minus the fur-covered dashboard).

Roads traveled.

I thought of this on the long drive to start vacation and smiled, a smile that did not last long as up ahead in the opposite direction I saw a sudden flash of emergency vehicles. Fire trucks. All southbound lanes were stopped, and as I slowed and got over to the right lane I could see the burned out shell of an SUV. There was nothing left but a charred husk, the fire so intense it had started a grass fire on the side of the road thirty feet away.

There was no other vehicle, it had not been hit, and it was in the right lane, not pulled off to the side. Something had happened fast and the vehicle was abandoned where it could be stopped. There was no ambulance or wrecker, I'd have seen it continuing south as I headed north. I could only imagine—engine fire? Fuel leak? Giant spare can of gas in the back (why people do that is beyond comprehension), windows up tight against the heat, fumes building and then poof? Spontaneous human combustion after a life of pork rinds and Big Macs? Many scenarios, none ending as planned.

After Mom died, I spent time at Dad's going through drawers and cupboards. In part it was to help my dad give to charity those things he did not need, but also to gather photos and mementos in one place for such a time when he could look at them again with joy, not anguish.

As any child does, we always picture our parents as being "old," as an image of staid authority and wisdom. Looking at the photos of my parents, growing up together, falling in love, I remember that although they invested an incredible energy in raising a family, they also invested an incredible energy in the things that made the two of them happy, outside of what was expected of them. What were they like, those two, before we came along? What dreams did they have that were denied, what dreams did they have that were unspoken?

Their lives certainly didn't travel as planned, a war interrupting their wedding plans for five years, the loss of a child followed by 11 childless years, then adoption. Then those children all traveling the world, family gatherings at best two or three times a year, Mom's health failing and Dad losing her so soon. It was likely not the life he'd planned on. Yet he kept on going, believing what he needed to believe or rather what was intolerable for him not to believe. He believed he would be happy again; and he was.

The traffic was moving along again, but at a pace of a three-toed sloth, not a sprint car. Up ahead, another slowdown: it looked like someone rear-ended someone, a minor accident given the speeds but worth getting off the freeway to get around on side roads.

I've known people through the years that have had every aspect of their lives planned and mapped out. The journey from birth to death laid out like a perfect roadway. Life, being something that refuses to cooperate with plans and possessing no map, usually throws them off on a different road, often without warning. It's how they respond to such detours that makes the difference between someone who simply survives and someone who sheds tears for the change but embraces the journey, finding happiness along the way.

I think back to more than one hunting trip, lying there on the cold ground, aching and sleepless under goose down as heavy as a lead apron, while my companions slept around me. I think back to those dreams that didn't go as planned. There in the wilderness where such senses are heightened I pictured life, fate, or whatever you call it, looming above like the dark canvas of tent, musing downward on this small cluster of fragile human dreams. I lay there thinking of all the times I hunted and came home empty-handed because I just didn't have it in me that day to take a life, not even for food; nothing to show for my exertions but unmarked solitude. Those were the days I remembered, where the deer pranced ahead of soundless guns and how the fierce sunlight of fall renewed me, even if I came home with nothing to show for my weariness but blisters and virgin ammo.

I'd then sleep and wake up renewed, walking out into the fields, the land flattened and calm, dissolving away under a cold rain like the rivers themselves dissolve away; and though I knew that however the day had ended I was here, alive. Over the years the ground got harder and the blankets a little rougher and thinner, but I was free to walk the land even as my shotgun was replaced with a camera. I was loved without expectation and I was loved deeply. Those were the gifts for which I was quite grateful.

As the wheels of my truck hummed along with the music and the traffic thinned out, I took the time to really look around me here on this side road I never expected to take. The landscape was warped and wrung in the heat into geometrical squares of wilted hope. The grass was dead, the trees bent down, limbs pulled against trunks as if hoping the sun would not notice them; the skeleton stalks of corn seeming to serve as warning to next year's plantings. The creeks were dry, the rivers thick and slow, almost without current. Yet in only a few months they would run wild again, spreading out over this land, drowning the fertile soil before subsiding again, leaving it richer even if it did not remain.

The trips to see my dad and now my daughter are good ones. The airfare back and forth ate a chunk out of our wallet and almost all of my vacation, but it was money and time spent gladly, my husband joining me when he could. Each time I went to Dad's, though, I was more and more aware that this could always be the last visit, and I know Dad was as well. Yet it didn't change how he looked at it. There were outings planned and board games dusted off, beer chilled and windows opened to the wind as if these summer days would go on forever.

Dad was just happy to have me home. He didn't bemoan the fact that I spent twenty years single again before finding a man who adored me as I him; the years too far gone to give him any grandchildren. He didn't mind that I carried a bag with a bodily fluid clean-up kit instead of diapers. He didn't judge that I often sat up late in the night, alone, reflecting back on roads taken; and how waiting patiently to live this life—as opposed to settling for one with someone for whom there was no affinity for me as an individual, only as a possession—was so much less lonely.

On such nights he didn't expect conversation or explanations, he simply brought me a mug of tea, kissed me on the forehead, gave my husband a hug and headed off to bed to dream those dreams that were still so alive to him. I would sit up until I knew he was resting comfortably, happy to hear the sound of his gentle snores, while he strode, as if young, through the fields of his youth, chasing immortal game that bounded ahead of his own silent guns.

Before slept I made the rounds of the house, inside and out. Out in the drive I placed my hand on the hood of the truck, feeling the residual warmth there under the rain's whisper; happy for the journey, however it took me to get here.

39

Tools for Life

There's a new grandchild on the way; no word yet if it's a girl or a boy. The children will be just a couple of years apart in age, like Allen and me. Rebecca is still bustling about, making patterns from scratch to sew the beautiful dresses she and my oldest grandchild wear. I'm not sure where she got that skill set from. I'd rather have a root canal than sew, but I'm perfectly happy making something in the garage, skills my dad passed on to me just as I'm sure her skills are ones her mom passed on to her.

Our relationship has evolved. I'm not Rebecca's mom, but I'm her other mother; and more importantly, I'm her friend. With her and her family, even the short visits every year and the phone calls and photos between, there are memories made, things she will remember and hopefully her children will long after I am gone.

I thought about that when I was visiting Dad recently. In his garage is a big fishing net; one that once held a mighty steelhead, now lying like a spent spider's web. In the corner a gallon jug full only of dust, with a homemade label that says "Geritol," a gag gift when one of my parents had turned fifty. I was in grade school, their adopting me late in life, but I recall a big glass jug full of some pink liquid and Mom holding it up and laughing, the sound of her voice like drops of rain.

Around Dad's shop I sweep up for him, seeing so many little bits of my childhood there: the leveler, the paint chipped away as if it had been in some sort of fender bender with the awl. Allen dug around one cabinet and found a cane from my tap dancing days to show to my husband, both of them now able to tease me—the top hat hopefully mercifully in hiding. Underneath the work bench was a small can of pink paint, the color of salmon that makes up the rainbow on my wall, the paint long dried up, the can a vacuum of the sharp smell of childhood dreams.

Just before we left Dad's on a recent visit, I did some general straightening up in his garage shop, laughing when I saw an old can of aerosol "BS Repellent" on the shop desk. What tools and machines lie in a garage speak a lot about the person who lives there as well as his skills. In my childhood home, if something electrical went south it was usually Mom who fixed it. It was the same for plumbing. It started when Mom was annoyed that the laundry room wall's cold and hot water faucets for the Maytag weren't seated well and would drip water down the paint, leaving a small puddle on the floor. Dad was enlisted to fix it. He did so by making little troughs out of foil in which the water ran away from the faucet and dripped into a bucket. Not onto the floor. When the bucket was brimming, the water would be poured out, thereby re-setting the system. Red Green would have been proud. Mom? Not so much.

But Dad could make anything out of wood. The fences around our family home, the storage shed, cabinets, and shelves, even a perfectly built A-frame playhouse for me in the backyard. Later, there was a deck which covered an area as big as two rooms, built when he was in his late seventies. It rose up around him as if a challenge to his age, strong as he still was, able to support the weight of the remainder of his life. He didn't use instructions; like anything else he created, he designed it on paper and made it himself. Everything would be perfectly tight, smooth, and proportioned, with a variety of wood to fit both form and function. His shop reflected those skills.

In most neighborhoods, the subdivisions anyway, walk down the road and you will see dozens of two- and three-car garages, most filled with junk and possessions to the point there is no room for a car, not even one car. There are few work benches to be seen. Instead there are "things"—those factory-made affirmations of deceptive immortality that one soon becomes bored with or that break. If something breaks, one doesn't search for a tool, one searches for a mall to go buy another one.

Too many people see the garage shop as simply something to be tucked away, a noisy and sometimes dirty place to which one can close the door. To me it's the house's most expressive feature, the tools of which measure the depth of its owner's true nature, the things crafted there, the design by which one perceived his life.

For some it's a way to be self-sufficient: to learn to build, repair, and restore, skills that could demand top dollar for which a budget would not allow. Such repairs were often done with tools purchased for the job, with books, or a computer from which to learn the skill. The joy was not in the task itself, but simply the affirmation that one can provide for the home, the family, with the work of one's own hands.

For others it's more than that. Walk into such garages, such shops, and it's a bit like an archaeological dig. When you walk in, you don't go back hours, you can go back generations. On the wall, a calendar from a year that is long gone, the pictures of trains on it the only reason it remains. On the floor, wood shavings and the occasional bit of metal, usually found when one makes that first and only mistake of venturing out there in stocking feet.

On the wall in Dad's garage there were tools, so many tools that pressed upon your brain like whispered words—telling you their stories of old pasts and new eternities, of what they had done, what they could do. Some people pick up such a tool, and it's the same feeling they get when they pick up a firearm: uncomfortable, cold, a necessity perhaps, or rather something to be discarded as soon as possible. To others, like myself, when they pick up such tools it means much more: that which places in your hand a weight; the heaviness of responsibility, the firmness of purpose.

For such people the shop is more than a little space tucked away behind closed doors. One some days, there in that place one's hands join in sensual dance with those hardened instruments, transforming rough materials by mind and imagination into some wonderful creation warped out of all experience. On other days, you simply end up with a new door stop. I'd not sacrifice either day for one spent watching reality TV.

On my garage work bench there usually sits a piece of wood, saved from becoming ashes to form something useful. Occasionally it's something metal, a piece, a part, one small component of something from which speed or safety can be derived. On another table, a large torque wrench simply known as *Excalibur*. If you can't bend it to your will, at least you can beat it into submission.

The skills involved, like anything of value, take time to learn, take patience. There would be mistakes. Some hopefully no more than a misplaced hammered blow, the hand curling up in pain like a leaf tossed upon a fire, perhaps a piece of wood or metal ruined due to your inattention or inexperience. There would be those projects where a friend or family member comes in and says without thinking: "Is it supposed to look like that?" But then comes that day when with the swing of that hammer or that hand on the lathe timidity and inexperience fall from your hands, and what you can make is not only recognizable in form, but serves a purpose, one that's unique to your life.

I enjoy hard work, so the thought of making my home in a hundred year old building was not daunting. With all the changes that have gone on around me, diving into a house whose final vision would require a bit of labor has taught me valuable things—and not just about budgets and planning, wood and nails and drywall. As I swung a crowbar one evening, working side by side with it, tearing out the damaged to replace it with the healed, the sweat from my face tasting like what I am, I realized that Dad didn't just teach me to use tools. He taught me to use the things that would teach me about myself.

Dad and I talk each night, but each and every week a bit more of him slips away from me, his mind now best functioning on a routine of days. I've found that when he is tired interrupting him sometimes confuses him, the phone taking him out of the place familiar to some imminent colorless dark he'd rather not think about. But then he recognizes the voice, though the name escaped him for a minute, and then he's my old dad again, if only for tonight. It's just part of having lived on this earth for ninety years, but it reminds me of how little time we have left.

So tonight I'll say a quick hello and let him get back to his shows on TV, the same ones he and Mom always watched. For him it's the routine of sameness that makes his night seem eternal, as if from the kitchen window that looks out onto the family room built on the old patio he could hear Mom say, "I'd like to buy a vowel!" Then I will pen him a letter, those notes he loves to get even more than the phone calls, for he can read them when he first wakes up, his mind clear, the world new. I will tell him how much the years have brought me, despite the struggles. I will tell him how I've learned to live on what is important, not some yuppified version of life, hollow and high priced. I'm satisfied, be it with the salty tang of a simple meal honestly made or the sweat on my brow from hard work.

So many times I thought I should tell him that as my tears mingled with the sweat of my task. I think now is the time.

I know there will come a time soon when I will have to clean out my dad's garage shop, that place where Allen and I played with trains on sheets of wood Dad had made and placed on sawhorses, painted green to be the landscape of our childhood. I will have to open that door into the space that is no longer used, peering into the shadows with eyes now silent with tears.

From a garage window, one that Mom covered with brightly covered vinyl to let in light while not allowing others to look inside, comes a ray of light, a stained glass hand upon the workshop. For just that instant I'm reminded of entering a church, the light of saints and angels held there in etched glass, looking down upon me, their faces young because they all die too young. I can only stop for a moment and bow my head in humility before proceeding inside.

Tonight I am away from my own home; but I can dream of it for I have no task than to do otherwise, studying a book of Mission style furniture designs, selecting the form of a small writing desk which will be crafted to be placed in a quiet corner. I search for just the right design, my form bent over the table like a question mark, the lines of the drawings like invisible threads that hold me to the past.

I know my dad cannot travel this far to see it when it is done, but I know he will smile at the thought. On the walls of the shop are tools that have seen three generations, tools that are still used. I pick up a household hammer that was my mom's. Even with remembered pain, I still can swing it strong.

Dad would like our home, my grandchildren will like this home, I think to myself as I pause from my task, a door to the outside world swinging shut in the wind while dark clouds are gathering above. From the window, a shaft of twilight, particle by particle borne by the rain and released within, the pale silvered blue of silk or sword blade. I study it in silence, the light both vision and benediction.

From outside there is only the muted sound of that brief rain shower, a soft *plop plop plop*, like drops of water falling into a brimming bucket.

40

A Fray in the Cord

When I was young, I mostly hung out with "the guys." I never fit in with the clumps of popular girls who giggled and posed and used their bodies to attract before they were even old enough to figure out what the attraction was. They clustered together in their own little gatherings in which dolls and accessories and small fluffy toys held sway. Their interests were foreign, and their forced interactions with me were tinged with derision. At that age their scorn had the finality of a curse.

My best friend was always my brother. Being adopted together, coming out of a less than ideal home situation, Allen and I bonded before we could speak. Mom and Dad had planned on just adopting one child, but life had had other plans for them.

Allen would often gently tease me; but we never argued or got angry with one another. Ever. For two redheads, that says something. There was a code between us—that we would always be there for one another and our parents, as if we both knew how important the bond of family can be.

He stuck up for me if kids were mean to me, and as an adult he bragged to his friends how cool his little sister was. We grew up and continued as survivors, he as a submariner and myself, a few years later, out playing with various aircraft that wanted to kill me. One of us underneath the sea, one far above; both of us drawn to the blue and to the precision of order and honor. Though as adults, even with much distance between us the bond remained strong.

That cord that connected us developed its first fray on September 11, 2001. Business sometimes took my brother to the Pentagon. I tried to call his phone but there was no answer, which was not unusual. It took me hours to verify his safety. Hours, because I was on alert myself, in a dark place that my education had prepared me to enter, but my innocence had yet to acknowledge was possible. But Allen was in another state that day, safe. My partner at work relayed the message that Allen was OK, and we were strong, invincible again.

Then there were the motorcycles. He was always big into riding. Myself not at first glance, having had not luck with neither men nor horses; but Allen said he'd show me how to ride safely, that he'd take care of me. He always took care of me.

We had many rides together, cruising the high roads, racing down steep grades just as we did as children on our bicycles, plummeting down fast and breathless as if banshees themselves were at our heels. I remember particularly one summer after our very last long ride together.

As the bikes idled in the driveway, in the light of his front headlamp Allen was suddenly surrounded by tiny bits of brilliance, a swarm of fireflies that we disturbed as we parked next to the grass. He put his face down to get a closer look and for a moment it was all I could see: his laughing in the glow of the headlamp, tiny bits of light rising up like little angels. Then, just as quickly, they moved away, leaving us there in the dark. With the darkness I felt an unexplained and inexplicable cold.

Months later I knew something was wrong before the phone rang. There was that chill again, tickling along the back of my neck, a heaviness at the base of my skull. I just knew. I called my dad to see what was wrong. Dad said all was fine as far as he knew.

Fifteen minutes later the call came in, my brother had been badly hurt—no head injuries thanks to the helmet and luck, but a lower leg was crushed, among other serious internal injuries. The cold stunned shock of it flowed through me like current, sorrow rising into questions. Where was he? Did he need blood? Was he aware? And a thousand miles away, in disbelief, I lay down on the bed and felt the pain of my inability to protect him.

After a round of surgery that stabilized him and six hours on airplanes, I was able to finally see him; hugging on the parts that weren't in a cast, feeling his large body so soft and weakened, as hard to hold as a snowman on that first spring day. In intensive care for Christmas, I bought him a tiny little crystal angel ornament that hung above the bed. It drew in whatever light could be gathered in that place, fragmenting them into tiny spots of light that shone around his face as he lay breathing, gathering strength as I simply sat next to him, praying the light would not fade. For if I could not be his little sister, who would I be?

But he survived, after almost a year in and out of hospitals and surgeries trying to save his leg, myself being there as often as I could. In later years, though we couldn't always be together, he'd find a way to remember; including a couple of years back when he came across a very old Christmas stocking with my name on it in ancient glitter. He filled it for me with things that he knew I liked and most people never would think of.

The next such call came on the afternoon of New Year's Day 2013. I'd been asleep, taking a nap as I'd not felt well earlier with a pounding headache that wasn't from a New Year's celebration. I had only had a single scotch and was asleep by 10:30 p.m. But I wasn't feeling right; and after I'd taken a casserole I made for a colleague playing single parent for a couple of days, I crawled into bed and slept for a couple of hours, only to be woken by the phone. I thought it would be a friend. Instead it was Dad—Allen was in the hospital. He had an "episode" while driving. A seizure or just passing out, they weren't yet sure. A friend who had been with him got them stopped and got him to the emergency room. Allen had lost a bunch of weight that year, saying he just had no appetite. He'd always been a tall, hefty guy, and he'd needed to lose about seventy pounds; but he attributed the loss of appetite to a change in his type II diabetes meds. He looked great with the weight loss and had no other complaints that we knew of. Apparently there were other symptoms—ones he didn't pass on, not wanting anyone to worry.

It was cancer, and it was in the lymph nodes.

I saw lights around my head, thinking for a moment of the fireflies. Then I realized I had just stood up too quickly, heart racing, not taking in a breath. I sat down slowly and looked around me at the photos of a young redheaded woman and her family, of my brother Allen and Dad; and I prayed to the Lord for their continued breath, for they are that extraordinary gift we often don't realize we have until they may be lost to us.

41

Friends

I saw this cartoon showing a funeral, the casket in the front of the church, and only one or two people in attendance. The minister is saying, "I'm surprised—he had so many Facebook friends." Social media is great and I've made several close friends there. But true friendship is most often found away from that computer screen, be it a phone call, a card, a visit; time spent in more than typing on a screen.

During his life, my black Labrador retriever Barkley and I spent a lot of time with friends.

The truck was loaded up with my bag, a cooler, some smoked salmon as a little gift, and dog supplies. Barkley was secured by his harness into the seat belt in the back seat in case of an abrupt stop. The harness did allow him to lie down, but he preferred to stretch out far enough to look into the front seat. He usually stayed that way the whole drive, occasionally leaning into me.

I was visiting my friends Mr. B. and his partner MC. We'd been friends for some years, meeting up at a gathering of mutual friends, myself just sort of all alone in the group, not knowing too many people. They had a black Lab. I had a black Lab. I like beer. They had a refrigerator full of beer in the garage, and MC and I would giggle like school girls when we were together. It was a friendship made in heaven, and one that has been one of my most enduring.

I remember one trip up there to visit while our elderly dogs played together. Traffic was picking up. We passed a company of bikers to whom I gave a friendly wave after I found a safe spot to pass the remainder of the group. I loved their leathers and appreciated the care, courtesy, and caution they were all using as they navigated a busy Saturday freeway. It was a pleasant drive, except for the sound of the furry demented air compressor behind me.

I arrived to the most wonderful smell wafting in from the deck. Mr. B. had one of his creations cooking away on the rotisserie, while in the kitchen MC, his partner of many years, finished up one of her homemade pies.

We got caught up while we nibbled, as it had been some weeks since we'd seen each other. This summer had just flown by, faster than any of us wished for. Their cats gathered around, including Bob who had been rescued during the winter, found freezing and starving outside of Mr. B.'s business. Bob remembered what it was like to be hungry, and even with care he seemed to be getting fatter and fatter even though he was on low-calorie cat food. We thought he was either stealing the dog food or drunk dialing the pizza place after everyone was asleep. I know he once stole and ate an entire waffle off my plate when my back was turned.

Whether it's in a home, at the local pub, or out at a local conservation club, there's just something wonderful about spending time with friends that know each other well. We know each other's quirks, faults, fears, and history; so much to draw from—conversations, pets, family, books, quips from movies. Conversations may be such that no one else can understand what we are talking about, times when just certain words bring about unrestrained laughter.

I brought out pictures of my two granddaughters—two beings that would not exist but for a choice I made long ago, in honor of the decision my parents had made. Mr. B. and MC dutifully looked at them and made the appropriate noises, for I *did* have a carving knife in my hand.

The meat was ready, the knife handed over to Mr. B. to cut servings with the delicate yet almost routine movements of the blade. Both their black Lab Schmoo and my Barkley looked up from the floor with that constant expression of incorrigible and hopeful expectation that is the devotion of a Labrador retriever.

We retired to the living room to settle in to digest, watch an automobile race, and make fun of the infomercials. You can't get a single channel up where Mr. B. and MC live that doesn't have this one particular attorney with bankruptcy infomercials, lots of them.

MC: "His mouth isn't moving in sync with his words."

Me: "Maybe that's just because he's an attorney."

Third or fourth commercial. . .

MC: "He's in sync now. How many years have these been on? Do you notice he never ages?"

Me: "I'm thinking he's Borg. Prepare to have your debt assimilated."

The race had started. Mr. B. was further explaining the art of braking and told a story of when he was racing flat track and used markers (a clump of grass or rocks) for judging where to start the braking in certain turns. During one particular race, while the car was still pointy end forward (but not for long), he set a track speed record. Apparently one of the rocks was a turtle—on the move.

This is friendship; this is what family means to me. Not necessarily the people we are related to, but those we let into our lives, to whom we expose our secrets and our faults. In the years since my daughter called me, my heart has opened up to these friends. I learned to love and trust again with their help and the eager wagging tail of my four-legged best friend.

My marriage is happy. I have connected to a daughter. That does not make up for the lost years, but it's a balm to my soul.

Future days may darken again, but I know they will always be here for me—to watch, to care, to listen.

For that is what friends do.

42

The Wind Chime

Allen had moved in with Dad after finishing his chemo and radiation. He couldn't afford his house anymore after losing his job during treatment. His son and growing family moved out of their small apartment to rent Allen's house instead so it would be cared for. Even better, Allen could now provide some companionship for Dad, lonely since the death of my stepmom, and his little dog long gone as well. Dad's health as well was starting to decline with normal aging, and I felt better knowing Allen was there if he needed something.

Of course, I'll forgive that trip they made to the hospital with Dad and a case of serious acid reflux because the two of them had sat out on the deck and each eaten a big jar of pickled herring, which they then washed down with beer.

My husband and I made another quick trip out to see them; and on arrival Allen took us out to the back deck where there was the melodious tinkling of a wind chime, something Dad and I both love. But this wasn't the usual cutesy "picked up at a beach gift shop" wind chime. This was something Allen had made while he was going through chemo and radiation. The treatment had been aggressive, as was the cancer; but Allen had needed something to focus on other than his own pain.

Like me, my brother doesn't like to sit still. So on the days he was well enough to get out, he'd pick up pieces of wood and what-not to add to his collection of things picked up from the beach. And when he was too weak to walk, he made wind chimes for family and friends.

There was a new one that had a sand dollar dangling from it by a cord. The sand dollar brought a knowing glance: we had picked up so many as children when we'd vacation on the coast each year in a tiny little cabin Dad and Mom rented. It's all condominiums now, but those were some great memories. From the looks of this sand dollar, it's one we picked up forty some years ago, those now lying in assorted bowls in all of our homes.

It hung outside my bedroom window as I lay awake at odd hours that week due to the jet lag. But as I lay quietly, the rest of the house asleep, I loved hearing the sound of that copper tubing, string, and ancient wood. I loved seeing it there on the deck where we could have coffee before Dad woke up.

You might only see a wind chime made of rough materials. I see a symbol of finding beauty in the face of that which severs you abruptly from the life you knew and did not wish to discard—thrust into a medium we are born to fear, where even our identity can be lost as hair and flesh fall away. I hear the sound of that which will never be forgotten. Memory. Family. Hope.

43

Time

In the morning's snow there were small tracks; some the bold steps of the predator, some the almost openly meek meanderings of a creature not yet aware it was prey. There were the sure steps of deer; another set of small fairy-like paw prints that simply ended, perhaps with a shadow and a mouth set in the "O" of pain that bespoke owl.

If you looked closely enough, you could see the narrative variants of the cessation of life—a tuft of rabbit fur, blood-speckled snow. Further on, a scattering of feathers, the type designed for speed intermingled with the downy innocence of plumage which had been designed for failed hiding, lying in a tiny crater of snow.

It seemed like only yesterday when summer was blazing. Now as I walked back to the house I shared with my husband, darkness approached even before dinner. Barkley was there at the door, the movement of his tail a tick against the time he waited for me.

We'd set our clocks back, we'd stopped saving our daylight. My day here, one late evening, lay under a blanket of night that began to thicken and bunch up around six, when just for a moment light hovered in an orb over the lake. Then with a blink it vanished up into the heavens, leaving just black exhaust in its wake.

The memory of that day comes back in the early mornings when the light creeps in too early and I still want to sleep, bringing with it the alarm of things to do.

Summer was here, and now it was gone—time passing much too quickly. On the wall, an anniversary clock of Mom and Dad's ticked, the evening light illuminating only its face so that it appeared to hang suspended in space. A ticking clock, holding in its hidden depths the regimented chaos of this world I've inherited, its ordered cadence the sound that moves me onward at a dizzying speed into a future still unperceived.

Two hundred years ago the days had their own measured order, as full and steady as the moon that rose each night in the sky. No one could have imagined today's electronic age, when time was taken from us and enslaved to a clock. Time changed from that of a fellow worker to an overseer, a sharp rap with a stick, a shrill alarm of warning.

Off in the distance I saw a train—stopped, yet with that sense of imminent departure that trains seem to possess. People no longer traveled much by train; we went in cars, faster and faster as roads got longer and days got shorter; driving to the market for our dinner instead of walking the land in search of game. The game itself had moved further inward, as had we.

In the dimming light I looked through some photos. There was one of me in the cockpit of a jet where I spent several years of my life pushing my limits. There was a photo of a piece of lace that helped make a wedding dress, one that I burned with the rest of the memories of that mistake. I got married so young and too soon, because I had a broken heart and thought a husband and perhaps another child would mend it. It only showed me how fixed the scars upon my heart were; and how unforgiving was he who saw them.

There were pictures—so many pictures of my brother and me. Allen was still my best friend, even after all these years. As adults, just as we did as children, we'd sit out at Dad's as we traced the stars with the beam of our flashlights. Not as a point in space, but a point in time—the pinnacle of childhood where morning and night and summer are one; the sleight of hand of fate and blood that would later shape us both so far distant as not to be conceived yet. Over the years, he pretended to not see some occasional tears; I pretended that I accidentally dropped the ice cube from my drink down his neck.

Years later another picture, a camping trip with Allen. We were out all day, heading in not by any clock but by the rhythmic cadence of breath and the measure of bone and muscle. The family dog was reluctant to come in from the water, "Just once more!" he seemed to speak to us. But our stomachs signaled dinner, and with a whistle we called him in. He came up the bank panting and trembling with the excitement of the day, to soft voice and gentle hand, seeking his pack.

Back in camp we settled to clean our fish and prepare our supper, hot coals lighting our work. Allen said grace to the communion of a small glass of whiskey and water, giving thanks for slightly burnt roast meat, a can of beans, and some bread that once actually resembled bread before it had seen my backpack, tasting of the outdoors. It was the best meal we all could remember eating in a long time, tasting of our labor and tinged with the smoke of our wildness.

The dog settled into sleep by the dying fire as in the darkness we prepared our bedding underneath an ancient sky. As the world slowly wound down, stars beginning to spin their stories in space, we talked. We talked of the world and its beauty, its love and its sin, where the words are our history, not other people's words which are not their past, but only the empty gaps of their days. We remembered Dad's stories of hunting as a boy in Montana when as children we lay quietly, listening to bedtime stories that knew no age limit; looking up at the quiet belly of canvas, hearing not a clock but only the measured breath of contentment as sleep brushed up the remaining crumbs of the day.

When was the last time you spent a day like that—with no clock, no schedule, just time with those that mean the most to you? Now, too often we rush and we scurry and we do not take the time to stop and think of the times we gave up—the times spent rushing after something we didn't really want or something demanded of us. Wasted minutes, wasted days.

Until suddenly years have passed, and the second hand poises in mid-second as you pick up the phone to make a call in the late hour. You pray he will answer—and in that instant all you register is the sound of breath and heartbeat, the phone held away from your ear. Outside, the rush of the wind; and somewhere far away the mournful sound of a train as you gaze at a photo of a young family on the wall, the red hair standing out like flame, waiting for him to answer.

You talk as you always did, as if nothing has changed from your shared childhood; but as you listen to him, you hear something else—the proverbial clock in your pocket. It's still ticking, more slowly, with a sound you never noticed before. Then with the moonlight reflecting off a tear that's forming, when you are certain the world is one still hush, you hear a bark from the backyard, Barkley the Labrador retriever, wanting to come in and sharing your time all that he asks for. So you set the phone down for a minute and open the door to call the dog in, as that happy bark fills the world with expressive tone, a measured tick of time. Time you both still have.

44

Running Silent and Deep

Friendships can form over many years of interaction. They can form in the sudden heat of battle. They can form over a handful of open, reflective conversations on or off the web—similar experiences, shared pain, among those who have earned your trust. They can involve humans, and they can involve four-legged friends who hold us just as dear, who protect us just as strongly.

All are valued.

I have one long-term friend who is very much like some of my friends, and beyond the conception of others. He's a couple years younger than me, never married, his whole life spent in service to our country including a trip or two to a war zone. Now he works in something that would be the stuff of a TV show if you could somehow narrow it down to an hour, throw in some cleavage, unrealistic outcomes of science, and the occasional bumbling probie.

But real life is not like that. Its not designer clothing while you assess the blood splatter, logical conclusions, or the good guys always winning. It's continuing to bear with weight and steadiness the evils and excesses of man, holding up strong under the business of the slain even when you might lose. Throw in a dress code and the occasional political yard gnome, and though we don't talk about it, we occasionally see something on TV and just look at each other and laugh.

He sometimes disappears for weeks or longer when I don't know where he is, and I know not to ask, though I've seen him on TV before. Then with a phone call out of the blue he pops in, occasionally on my front porch.

My husband understands our long history and that bond, and just smiles a wry smile while the guest bed is made up and my friend and I have animated conversations involving Bosnian goats, wrong way tanks, and various shiny aircraft. For it is a friendship that is like family, even though we don't share blood or any sort of romantic history—just a lot of years, some mutual skirmishes, a number of fish sandwiches and pints, some bullets, and a passport or two.

Then there were the friends of childhood. Often such friendships didn't survive high school as we grew and evolved into the people we would eventually be. One such person was the girl who lived across the street. She was my best friend in grade school; a tiny little thing with ice-blond hair. When we were kids, her little sister died of a rare form of cancer, then her still-young mom of the same disease. Her dad soon followed, though we're not sure if it was disease or heartbreak. She and I lost touch after high school, the friendship being more one of young girls than grown-ups.

We went off to college, myself initially majoring in engineering, my friend doing pre-med. I heard later she ended up working for a medical research facility. She studied the disease that had laid its cold hand on her family, hoping for a cure, likely looking at it each day with both horror and astonishment. Unfortunately, the disease took her before she could take it. She was only in her thirties, the world to her still comprised of small wonders.

We hadn't had contact in years, and it was months after she passed that I heard. She had no living family left; nothing remained of her but the handcrafted wood that held her remains. So small, so bare. That's really all that life ends up as, I thought, and my heart swelled with tears—for the girl she'd been, for joyous laughter watching cartoons, for whispered conversations about who liked what boy, for afternoons at ballet class; for all the joy and adventure we had as we explored our world with a curiosity and courage that had not learned limits. I cried with the realization that we had both let that slip past us, unremembered over so many years.

All I could do was go to the church and light a candle for her, then blow on it to release the flame, releasing her laughter with it, and the memories of childhood.

If we are fortunate, those we live with are also our friends. My dad married his best friend, as did I. I look at other friends of mine long married and I see that, and it's precious to behold just being in the same room with the two of them; sitting across the table as we say grace you can feel the flame.

There's nothing better than sharing a last name with your best friend.

Growing up, my big brother Allen was the best friend a kid could have, his not abandoning me even in high school when it just wasn't cool to hang out with your baby sister. But lately we'd gotten much closer.

Because he was dying.

He had kept the truth from our ninety-four-year-old father, hoping that he would outlive Dad, sparing him that agony. But I knew even if he didn't tell me, having too much knowledge of medicine not to understand what was going on. But I did everything I could to spend as much time with Allen during those last six months. In his last months on this earth we'd talk of everything: about our dad, about growing up (or our inherent refusal to). One thing I am glad was that I never heard from him during those conversations, "I wish I'd . . ."

I've heard so many people say: "I'll do that when I'm older, when I lose twenty pounds, when I'm retired." We go through life saying, "I would, but it probably wouldn't work out," or, " I'd like to but . . ." We too often base our actions on an artificial future, painting a life picture based on an expectancy that time is more than sweat, tears, heat, and mirage.

You can't count on anything. For out of the blue fate can come calling. My husband and I had recently lost our beloved black Lab Barkley after a brief but valiant battle against bone cancer and a weekend of pain we couldn't keep at bay for him. In a flash life robbed me even of the power to grieve for what is ending. I think back to when Allen and I were kids: going down a turbulent little river with little more than an inner tube and youth, risking rocks and rapids and earth just to see what was around the bend of that forest we'd already mapped out like Lewis and Clark. The water was black and silver, fading swirls of deep current rising to the surface like a slap, fleeting and gravely significant—as if something stirred beneath, unhappy to be disturbed from its slumber, making its presence known. A fish, perhaps; or simply fate.

I think of the true story of the woman whose parachute didn't open on her first jump and she fell more than a mile, and lived—to change her whole life to pursue her dreams. Did she sense something as she boarded that plane, looking into the sky at a danger that she could not articulate that she could not see? Or was she unaware until that moment when she pulled the cord and nothing happened, as her life rushed up to her with a deep groaning sound? What was it like in that moment, that perception of her final minutes, what taste, what color, what sound defined her soul as it prepared to leave?

I was in the paint section of a hardware store the other weekend, looking for a brick-colored paint to spruce up a backdrop in the crash pad's kitchen. I noticed the yellows, the color I had painted my room as a teen. I noticed the greens, so many of them—some resembling the green of my parents' house in the '60s and '70s, yet not being exactly the same color. The original was one that you'd not see in a landscape, only in a kitchen with avocado appliances while my Mom sang as she made cookies. I remember Allen and I racing through the house, one of us soldier, the other spy, friends forever; stopping only long enough for some of those cookies, still warm. Holding that funky green paint sample I can see it as if it were yesterday. Memories only hinted at, held there in small squares of color.

What is it about things from the past that evoke such responses? For some it's a favorite photo; a piece of clothing worn to a special event; a particular meal. Things that carry with them the sheer impossible quality of perfection that has not been achieved since. Things that somehow trigger in us a response of wanting to go back to that time and place when you were safe and all was well. But even as you try and recapture the memory, it eludes you, caught in a point in your mind between immobility and motion, the taste of empty air, the color of wind.

One morning while out in a hangar checking out a pilot friend's home-built project, I had one of those moments. It was an old turboprop lumbering down the taxiway with all the grace of a water buffalo. It wasn't the aircraft that caught my eye, it being one of those planes that carries neither speed nor sleek beauty, but rather serves as the embodiment of inertia overcome by sufficient horsepower. No, it was the smell of jet fuel that took me back—to years of pushing the limits, not really caring if I came home, only that the work was done without my breaking beyond re-use something I was trusted with.

Until one day, while my heart was beating despite being broken unseen beneath starched white cotton, my aircraft made a decided effort to kill me. It was not the "Well, I'll make a weird sound and flash some red lights at you and see what you do," an aircraft's equivalent of the Wicked Witch of the North cackling: "Care for a little *fire*, Scarecrow?" No, it was a severe vibration that shook the yoke right out of my hand as we accelerated through 180 knots on the initial climb when, unbeknownst to me, a small piece of metal on the aircraft's tail had come loose and was flapping in the breeze.

In that moment, as I heard the silent groaning of the earth below, I thought: I do not wish to die—and I fought back. In that moment of slow and quiet amazement that can come at the edge of sound, finding in myself a renewed desire to live; recognizing the extent and depth of that desire to draw another breath and share that soft warm breath with another.

Today is a memory that months from now could be one of those memories—not of fear, but of triumph. You may look back and see this day, the friends you were with, the smile on your face, the simple tasks you were doing together. Things, so basic in their form to at this time simply be another chore: cleaning, fixing, an ordinary day; while children played with a paper plane fueled by laughter and the hangar cat drowsed in the sunlight. It might be a day you didn't even capture on film—no small squares of color left to retain what you felt as you worked and laughed together, there in those small strokes of color, those small brushes of hope as you wait for your best friend to join you.

Twenty years from now you may look at yourself in the mirror, at the wrinkles formed from dust, time, and tears around your eyes, at the gray in your hair; and you will think back to this day, the trivial things that contain the sublime. On that day, so far beyond here and now, you may look around you, that person you were waiting for no longer present, and you'll want it all back. Want it as bad as the yearning for a color that is not found in nature, in the taste of something for which you search and ache, acting on the delusion that you can recreate it, those things that haunt the borders of almost-knowing.

You touch the mirror, touch your face and wish you'd laughed more, cared less of what others thought, dove into those feelings that lapped at the safe little edges of your life, leaped into the astonishing uncertainty.

Allen spent years running silent and deep under the ocean, visiting places I can only guess at as he will not speak of it, a code about certain things I share with him. But I knew the name. Operation Ivy Bells. He understood testing the boundaries of might and the cold depths to which we travel in search of ourselves.

On his last nights, Allen and I talked, but not of those days under the ocean. We both were aware of grave matters of honor, but do not speak of them, not even with each other. I'd sit as he talked about Dad and how he hoped Dad would live to be a hundred; how he hoped he would be there to take care of him, even as I watched 120 pounds leave Allen's frame as he went through that second round of chemo and radiation.

He talked until his eyes closed, only his labored breath letting me know he was still with me; the rise and fall of his chest as he were trying to push up from the waters of the sea, unfathomed flesh still so buoyant if only in spirit as the cold water lapped against him.

I too have had more than one day where I stood outside on a pale crescent of beaten earth and breathed deeply of that cold. On those days I felt every ache in my muscles; my skin hot under the sun; the savage, fecund smell of loss in the air, lying heavily in the loud silence. Somewhere in the distance would come a soft clap of thunder; overhead clouds strayed deliberately across the earth, disconnected from mechanical time. I'd rather be elsewhere; the smell simply that of kitchen and comfort: the sounds only that of laughter. But I knew how lucky I was to simply *be*, in that moment, and alive.

I'd go home on such nights and pour a drink, prepare a small meal. I'd eat it slowly, letting the sweet and salt stay upon my tongue. For me there would be no quick microwaved meal eaten with all the detachment of someone at a bar, tossing back a handful of stale nuts with his beer. No, I wished to taste and savor the day, the warm layers of it, this day that had been someone's last.

You can't control fate, but you can make choices. You can continue your day and do nothing, standing in brooding and irretrievable calculation as if casting in a game already lost. Or you can seize the moment, the days, wringing every last drop from them. Tell the ones you love that you love them. Hug your family; call an old friend you've not spoken to for months; forgive an enemy; salute your flag—and always, *always* give the dog an extra biscuit. Then step outside into the sharp and unbending import of spring, a dying winter flaring up like fading flame. One last taste, one last memory, never knowing how long it will remain.

As I sit and wait for the phone to ring to let me know my husband has landed, I have no idea what this day will bring as it closes. But one thing I do know: today *is* that memory. Alone or together, I'm going to go out and make everything I can of it. I look at the photos of Rebecca and her family, drawings my granddaughters made. I look at a photo of Allen, the shirt he wore in the last picture I have of him now hanging in my closet, next to a crisp cotton shirt that still bears the scent of memory. I pause and smile, preparing my evening table with thanks to the Lord for the blessing of family and friends.

45

The Depths of a Heart

I was out at Dad's again, making my trip to the garage as I always do. The car was gone, given to a family member who needed one when Dad wasn't able to drive any longer. In its former space were boxes and boxes of a life, all of Allen's things carefully packed for his children to take, most of the clothes going to charity. A few pieces of his submarine memorabilia sit on my dresser now; the rest simple, silent shadows. Still, I can see past them to what was there so long before.

I stayed just long enough to take the trash to the barrel outside and to check the freezer to see if I needed to buy Dad some more ice cream. It was hard to see inside, my eyes misty; breathing in the bracing density of cold air laced with pine and motor oil, a smell I loved even after all those years. It was the smell of morning's breath, full of wood and silence.

Before I closed the garage door I stood for just a moment, looking deep into this familiar space, out onto the driveway shaded by Mom's old tree. For just a moment, the boxes were gone from my vision, replaced by a memory of hands and tools and laughter. I could almost see my big brother there; the shifting green shimmer of persistent leaves creating an illusion of shadow, of form within, working away until Mom called us in for supper.

It was in that driveway he finally collapsed, tending to Dad as we both have always done. We later asked ourselves if he'd tended more to himself and less to the family, had he shared the pain he was hiding, would he have had a few months longer? But that's just who he was, always a submariner, always on quiet watch; the risk and the fear of death second to those things which men store within the depths of a human heart.

That he left me just weeks after we laid our black Lab Barkley to rest, also to cancer, hit me even harder.

The tragedy was not that my brother was gone so soon, but that he was no longer here to see what remained—the hearts he repaired, the things he built that can't be contained in one's hands. Allen went full speed up to the end, not wanting to extinguish his thirsting heart but only to slake it.

As I stood on the step from garage to laundry room and pushed the button for the garage door, I took in the sight, the smell of it. I couldn't imagine Allen not being here; something that just *is*, like the loud *crack* of a bat hitting a ball; the bounce of a bicycle off the gravel as kids came careening into home; the way an old baseball game seeped out of a transistor radio as a loved one worked away. Sounds that echoed even as the door closed and darkness descended.

46

Scars but No Regrets

My husband and I were making progress renovating our new house. Well, "new" was stretching it. If this house was a rescue dog it would be a senior—and even that was a stretch since it was almost one hundred years old. But it was home.

It wasn't home like where I had grown up, that place where my brother Allen and I ran and played in the endless rains of summer; where in winter we built forts of white and tumbled through the drifts like glacial stones. In snow gear of jeweled hues we played until we were forced to come in; harnessing the earth's energy, keeping our childhood alive.

It was hard yet rewarding work. But I enjoyed laboring alongside my husband, pulling cabinetry out of the wall, taking tools and making them do what I needed, the sweat on my forehead reaching my mouth, tasting of who I am, someone who's worked hard for everything she's got—someone who will raise some sweat to keep it. When I bought the house I owned before I met my husband, it also needed a lot of work, like bathroom fixtures and an updated kitchen; and I did most of the work myself. I worked late into the nights alone, too many nights using leverage to swing the tools—but at times it seems like there were two of us, the tools and I working side by side like familiar lovers who can guess each other's moves, hearts speaking to one another in musical measures beyond the need for words.

Some of the work I was proud of; some of it made me thankful for throw rugs and large pieces of art. But like farm living it kept me centered, close to the ground, to the earth and blood and fluid need in all things. It also honed my swearing in Norwegian, for which my grandfather would be proud.

The tools I have are old and precious to me, some given by friends, some from home. Tools my Dad used to craft the fence around his own house, the detailed and geometrically perfect cabinets in his garage. Tools that have stood the test of time, held by three generations; tempered by fire and heat to be strong under stress, and having enough flexibility to get out of corners and swing freely as needs arise. Just as he raised us to do.

I learned about hard work early on, facing it like battle to which you carry ancient wounds. You can't live on a farm or a ranch without learning about hard work. I spent ten years as a young bride living such a life with my former husband so long ago. I know the signs of impending birth in a heifer. I know how to cut a single longhorn from a herd of fifty with nothing but an ATV and a dog, all while avoiding the pointy ends. I didn't compare nail polish colors with my girlfriends, because long fingernails sort of get in the way when you might have to grease a cupped hand and naked arm with Betadine and lubricant to help a breached calf make its way into the world. I've fallen face first in stuff you don't want to know about, and cried like a child to find a calf still and cold after I spent two days nursing her after her mama died.

It wasn't *Green Acres*; though I think we had their house. It had nothing to do with Norman Rockwell and everything to do with the hundreds of different ways a heart can freeze.

It was a valuable lesson in life. Hard work, hard decisions, made on evenings like that one years later as I worked away at my home, listening to the sound echo in an empty house, learning about life and love with all the salt and truth one can expect from the swing of a hammer. It taught me more than how when physics and your thumb meet, your thumb will lose; it taught me about budgets and planning, woods and nails and drywall. It taught me what I have the capability for, and it taught me to dream the dreams of a child again.

As my husband and I pulled an old decaying lattice away from the side of our house, I had to stop and sort my words as memories came unbidden—color, movement, shape. The first was of my mom bending over the garden, helping my dad weed; a good woman over whom death had already cast its shadow as surely as the apple tree shading her that day. Our rescued wiener dog mix Pepper pranced around her in play, barking joyously. Standing there in that barren flower bed a lifetime later, I could still smell her perfume on the air; I could hear that bark and the remembrance of the fluid movements of her hands in the soil was as real to me as a tide. Gentle, measured, certain.

I think back to the days on the farm, to another house, and I remember not the hard times but the good. I remember the last winter there, when I helped a neighbor pull a reluctant calf from his mother's womb. If I close my eyes, I can relive that next moment in which I ceased to breathe myself as the calf did not. In that moment all I could I hear were the tiniest sounds, the fairy feet of barn mice and the creak of a rafter. Then in a rush of indignation came the mighty and protesting bawl of that newly-born bull calf, his cries from a birth-wet mouth awaking something in his weary mother who lay so still there under the dark moon, both of us totally spent from the effort. I still can picture his trusting eyes fixed on her as she rose up to sniff and take him in with that wonderful snuffling devotion of a mother.

Our memories are not the house we live in. They are inside of us, all of those memories, the laughter and sharing of friends, all of the fun and adventures that will follow us home. Home is the pillow on which you lay your dreams, brought out with just a word, a sure and steady gentle touch.

Tomorrow will be the long drive home, after a long week of work. When I get there it will just be getting dark. I will replenish supplies, taking out an empty dog food sack to the trash. The driveway will lie in a placid warm slumber, silent under my feet. I'll pull closed the back door, looking at land that holds neither corn nor cows, seeing the rise of another old house in the distance as I begin a clog-stomping run back onto the porch. The chilling night air whistles through my shirt, tickling skin, scorching my bare cheeks and the back of my throat.

Inside the door, where the mailman pushed it through, lies a letter from a foreign land. The handwriting looks almost like him: slender and strong and focused. I can almost smell the scent of gin and tonic as I tear open the envelope and drink in the words. Those words are water to me, the paper a quiet pool, myself merely one of those little water bugs that lie not quite on the surface nor beneath it—but in that quiet line of demarcation that is neither water nor air, earth nor heaven; exposing to the outside world only what is necessary to draw breath and hope.

Soon, there in that house I never expected to be, it is time for bed. There on the nightstand is a dried maple leaf, a candle, a couple of framed photos. I lie back across the edge of the bed, naming off each vertebra; looking upward as my body stretches downward, long red hair trailing to the floor like a line of fire. On the floor is an empty dog bed. Perhaps it's time for another dog, I think. I smile up at stars that glitter like mica through the window, at unheard poetry that hides on the dark side of the moon, at the sun that warms another pillow far away; thankful for the journey here, however painful.

I may have my scars, but I have no regrets.

47

Moving On

My husband and I had retrieved the rest of the things to be moved from my home to his. There was a box of dog toys on the porch which I couldn't bear to open. We had talked about getting another dog, looking at reputable breeders, checking ads; but I didn't think I was ready, waiting for a sign perhaps.

That night as we went to sleep I dreamed of my old dog Barkley, something I'd not done in several months.

In my dream life hasn't changed; Allen and Barkley are still with me and it's just a normal day of prayer and reflection.

On the wall is a crucifix, symbol of blood and wind, strength that follows me through my day.

As I enter the building, the light shines on those small testaments of ritual, those things that bring peace and beauty to what could otherwise be chaos. A drape of white cloth upon which lies a cup; a candle there, unlit for now but soon to be anointed by flame.

I know he's waiting for me so that I can unburden myself. He's probably thinking as well, it's been so long since I've been back. I wait outside the door for just a moment, taking in the tranquil quiet, the peaceful shadow.

But first I will light the candle, for me, for souls unlit. For the ones I could save and those I could not, all merging now into one sustained breath that ignites this small candle into flame. The flame swirls up unto the heavens as the stars bow and draw backwards.

In my pocket are forgotten implements. I gently finger them like beads, uttering the words that came from my mouth as I worked with them, words that strung out like coronals of roses as I disturbed another's solemn remains, bent and bowed to my duties. Forgive me. Forgive them.

I pull those tools of my day from my pocket and lay them upon the white cloth. In the candlelight they gleam like the nicked and scuffed chain mail armor of angels.

From behind the door I hear the murmur of movement as my arrival is sensed. I stand outside, as silent as I did not long before, tongues of ash and flakes of fire raining down, anointing the bones of men. How I wish they would stir, awakening to the fire, but they sometimes do not. I make the sign of the Cross, peace to their ashes.

I open the door, but it is not the door to penance and confession, not at this hour, this place. But it is a door to one that still, with heart untouched by either sin or evil, will listen to me even if he cannot speak.

He will listen as liquid words flow from weary brain, symbols that are not of a periodical, but of the elements of mystery; questions asked and reasoning answered. He will listen without asking and he will forgive without penance, though he can be stirred to almost evangelical zeal by a small nugget of biscuit.

From the distance, a church bell—a sound that does more than note another hour, one more increment of time and grief that's ticked since Genesis. It's the sound of hope and faith, one that cleaves the air with a sharp instrument of promise as a dog joyously barks.

For it is not a man of a cloth I was unburdening myself to, but my best friend Barkley the Labrador retriever.

When he has eaten first, I will go out to sit at that cloth-covered table. I will take the meat, the bread, and the wine and I will pause, bent with sin but saved by Grace, there as I bow my head in thanks. It is thanks not just for the company of friends and the reminder of hope—but for a small furred creature who blessed me with the wag of a tail.

I awoke with tears on my face and the comfort of words in my head.

I think it is time to add another dog to this home. This time it's going to be a rescue, a dog that needs a home as much as we need him.

48

Abby the Rescue

I asked our veterinarian about some reputable rescue organizations and got a couple of names. We wanted another Labrador retriever—not to replace Barkley, as you can't exchange one soul for another that easily; but they are such good and gentle dogs, and from the looks of things there were a number locally that needed good homes. There were some purebreds available as well as some pups and younger dogs. My husband told me to pick whichever I wanted.

I saw the web page of one of their older dogs, one who'd been in a shelter for months, left heartworm-positive. She was gray around the muzzle in the photo from her foster home and smaller than Barkley ever had been. Her fur was longer, the tail bushier, some other breed than Lab in her. She would be available when her heartworm treatment was done. Her name was Abby.

I filled out the adoption paperwork, made arrangements for the Lab rescue folks to see my home, either in person or through photos. As I worked in one state and lived in another there were two homes still, a small crash pad for work and the home I shared with my husband. Both were away from the road with a small yard and parks nearby for walking.

It took a few weeks. I was interviewed, and the rescue people called three references.

Abby's foster mom brought her over to the crash pad after I got off work. Abby was shy and a little thin, but she was affectionate and pounced on some toys I had bought with gentle glee. She didn't leave the house again; we finalized the adoption right then and there for a small fee to cover some of her costs and the microchip and vet information for my records.

Our first day went very well. I got up once in the night and Abby came in from the furry rug in the hall that she had chosen over the dog bed. She made sure I was OK, and then went right back to sleep.

When I woke up that morning it was to a happy face and: "Oh boy, it's dog food again!"

After a walk, Abby doing well with the pulling but sometimes weaving ahead (actually more like dropping down immediately in front of me like a driver in a NASCAR race), which I had been warned about by her foster mom, I made an appointment for dog training. Part of the adoption agreement was that I would get her basic training, and I planned on honoring that—to work on the leash skills and any other basic commands she needed to work on, though she'd come when I called and sat on command. I then made an appointment with our veterinarian, Dr. H., for a general wellness exam, to get all of Abby's information into the system and plan out any care she might need over the coming months.

Abby did great in my truck and wasn't at all anxious at the vet. She even calmly laid down while we waited in the exam room about ten minutes (we were quite early). Barkley not only would *not* have laid down, he'd have been rifling the cabinets for prescription dog treats. Abby just quietly waited on lead, right there on the floor.

She was great with the exam other than squirming when it was time for the ears, as all dogs do. Follow-up care for her heartworm was discussed as well as a Lyme screen, as she had evidence of a possible recent tick bite. Barkley had loved Dr. H., and Abby was no different, trying to give her "kisses" on the face to the point I heard a laugh and "No tongue!" Abby got a new prescription for her monthly heartworm and flea medication, and I purchased enough for a few months. After pats and treats from Dr. H. and her gentle and skilled assistant, we were on our way home.

After we got to the house I had an errand to run to the grocery store, and Abby did really well on her own while I was gone for an hour. The master bedroom bed wasn't slept on, she hadn't chewed on anything; but she was happy to see me, though not anxious. I was glad I had taken a few days of leave from work for Abby's first few days here. My husband would come down the next couple of weekends so she could get used to him before seeing her other home.

At the store I bought her one of those frozen dog treats. Barkley loved them and would delicately lick them until they were gone, on a plate. I expected the same from gentle Miss Abby.

I put the treat on the plate sans container. She sniffed and tentatively licked it, then . . .

You know that scene in *Jaws* where the shark grabs the guy whole in his mouth and swallows?

It was something like that. That was one happy dog! Though how she kept from getting brain freeze is beyond me.

I couldn't wait for my husband to meet her.

49

Lifespan

I tried to visit Dad as often as I could in those first weeks after we lost Allen. Dad wished to remain living in his home, so a home health nurse was hired to provide full time in-home care and drive him where he needed to go. I had mentioned his getting another dog—but he was having difficulty standing up, so a dog that had to be let out would probably not be a good idea.

But Dad has had a number of rescues over the years, the last being a Dalmatian named Ashley. When he got her he was ninety and the dog was almost twelve. There was no telling who would outlive whom; but he was so happy to have that four-legged friend to share his big old house with.

But with good quality food and regular veterinary care, Ashley the Dalmatian lived two very comfortable years with him; and Dad at ninety-four is doing better than average.

Think about it. As a society we now live decades longer than our ancestors. I remember reading the book *Alaska* by James Michener; in the opening chapter, there in the dawn of time they speak of "the Ancient One," a woman who was a great healer and spiritual leader. She was in her thirties. Oh great, I thought as I read it, first the big three-oh, now I'm ancient.

These days most of us can expect to live well into our seventies and eighties, some even into their hundreds. Yet some creatures live only months or even days.

Late one fall a cricket moved into my garage of the crash pad. Night after night he chirped away on the other side of my bedroom wall. Leaving the garage door open a bit didn't encourage him to leave, only to have a party with some of his bigger friends. I was able to shoo them out, but he hopped into a little crack to hide so he could continue to serenade me. After a few nights of that I was wondering as to ways to dispatch him. (Would using a silencer on a cricket be illegal or apropos?)

I did a little checking online—apparently the life span of the average field cricket is just a *couple of months*. Already an adult, he likely had only a few weeks to live, if that.

The poor little guy wouldn't even make it to Halloween; but each night he sang as if he would live forever. I didn't have the heart to capture him and move him outside. He could stay safe in my garage as my pet cricket. I named him "Mort."

Consider the hummingbird: such a small creature with such a high metabolism, yet it has a life span much greater than you'd think, with some living more than a decade. I watch them from the feeders in summer, warring for the liquid nectar found within, fending off others that wish to take it; watching, guarding, always wanting more of life's sweetness. No different than what we want.

I think of lives cut short that achieved so much for their brief time here, like my favorite poet John Keats, who threw over medicine to write some of the most sublime odes in the English language and died at twenty-five from tuberculosis; Percy Shelly; M.F. Xavier Bichat, French army surgeon turned pathologist; Évariste Galois, mathematician and inventor of group theory who died at twenty; Robert Fergusson, Scottish Poet; Saint Albertus Magnus. Their words, their teachings still follow me where I go, whispering to me in unexplored depths or darkest of nights—such great thoughts tinged with wonder and mystery, those whispers of slain genius.

Fortunately our human life span is much longer than most creatures'—if we are blessed and take care of ourselves. But even the greatest expanses of time seem so short in recollection. Walking through the little village where I live, the sidewalk glinted with little bits of mica. Not the prophet Micah, but the geological kind. As a kid, the sidewalk would glitter like broken glass upon the tide flats from the small glints of mica within it. Allen said it was made of broken starships, and I believed him. For though there are limits to what we may accept as children, there is no limit to what we can believe, nourished as we are by the embrace of the incredible that is found right beneath our feet.

Into the warm days of fall that is childhood's longest hour, in those weeks of summer vacation we believed we'd live forever. We weren't content just to ride our bikes on these glittering trails of star-stuff; we'd get big pieces of chalk and drew on them, hopscotch, tic-tac-toe, our names. We'd play well into the dark, coming in only when we were hungry, the front doors unlocked to our comings and goings—time for us was something we could pick up and put in our pocket.

When I go home and my brother's laughter is silent, there is no weather of distance between that time and now. It seems like yesterday. But I have realized that the saying is true: man does carry his life in his hand. My dad's siblings, though blessed with a hardy disposition, also possessed an intrepidity of spirit and courage that might have been called reckless in others; but in them it was a natural trait when tempered with a soundness of choice. They honored their bodies as vessels of God and didn't abuse them with drugs or an excess of alcohol or even food. In the pictures I have of them together I see only lean, honed strength and purpose of duty.

I look at a collection of bones on a table, beautiful to me in their pristine immobility. I look at a glass box Aunt Marion left me that sits on my desk. In it is *Urania ripheus*, more commonly known as the sunset moth, hovering on lifeless wings that glow in the light as if lit aflame. The sunset moth is found on the shaded areas of river banks in Madagascar. The essence of life floats elusive, half submerged in the waters of science, buoyed by God. I've spent the last fifteen years studying the many tragic ways life ends; and still I draw great comfort from the way it fights to remain.

Somewhere a thousand miles away, meal time drawn to a close, Dad will be in his recliner reading that old family Bible, the book for all the days remaining. Dad never knew his destiny would be to live to great age, to love deeply, outliving two children and two wives. A love that entranced him and made him its own to the most secret of thoughts, to the disquiet of blood, to his last exhalation. He did not know his destiny, but he followed it with unfaltering footsteps. The Bible is gently laid in his lap as he nods his head for a nap. The winter window fades, then glows—a living spark there among the shadowed embers, as at his feet lies an empty dog bed.

50

Taking Abby Home

After almost two weeks at the crash pad—my husband coming to stay with us last weekend so Abby could get used to one place a bit before uprooting yet again—it was time to take Abby back to our home, where hopefully I'll live full-time in the next year or so as I look into a job transfer. Most of my belongings had been moved to our home, keeping just enough in this little place to be cozy and comfortable on the days that I worked.

One of the traits I looked at when picking a dog to adopt was "Rides well in the car"; as, like Barkley, she would commute with me each week as I made my way to the city at my job in another state.

I decided to leave in the morning. I was really tired from a long week, and there was thunder and hail going strong as I left work on Friday. I also I thought Abby would be more relaxed driving in the early morning when she was still a little sleepy. We'd made a few short drives this last week, and she took well to the harness system. The harness allows her to sit and lie down in the back, but not move forward or turn into missile dog in the event of the accident. Saturday morning dawned with good weather, everything was packed up. This should be a breeze.

I woke up to find Abby with her head in the food bowl—not the little one but the BIG one, the plastic container that holds forty pounds. Apparently Miss Abby figured out that if Mom doesn't latch the top down tight, she can snoot the lid up and have herself a little snack off of the top. And she did, on top of her regular breakfast. There wasn't a whole lot missing, a couple of cups perhaps; and her belly wasn't hard—so I figured she'd be full but OK.

Until I got out of the shower to find out she'd barfed on the only really expensive rug in the house. I swore Barkley was up in doggie heaven giving her pointers somehow.

I got that cleaned up and took her out to potty, but she really didn't have to go—so we loaded up. I knew she was a little nervous as we got in the truck because the last time she made a long trip, she ended up in another strange place with very kind but new people. After several months in a shelter and being treated for heartworm, that had to have been scary for her.

So I kept my eye on her. Having always had family dogs, I know about the effects of overeating, mainly, "dogrrhea." She seemed just fine when we left the crash pad.

But as we hit every pothole on the interstate going north, she started to get a little restless. One moment she had been happily sleeping, and then she suddenly sat up, maneuvered, and let loose an explosive spray from her back end that would have done a demolition team proud.

I didn't think a little dog could hold that much.

We got off the road at a nearby rest stop. I didn't scold her—she couldn't help it. Instead I patted her and got her cleaned up as best I could (thank you, paper towels and a garbage bag in the emergency road kit). Then I wiped down the seat and the floor (most of it had hit the floor and the back of my seat). I then went into the rest rooms to get cleaned up. One woman wrinkled her nose at the smell (my jacket sleeve got hit) and I just said, "You should have seen the other guy!"

I called my husband and told him I'd be a little late. We took another walk, making sure Abby was completely empty before getting her some fresh water and a blanket. From then on she was all happy with no further discomfort for the rest of the drive—though I was seriously tempted to stick my ear plugs up my nose, having left the Vicks in my work bag.

Despite the smell I was getting hungry and stopped for a roast beef sandwich. Not only did Abby look interested, she gave me this look that said, "Has anyone told you that large quantities of cow can restore an electrolyte imbalance caused by dogrrhea?"

When we rolled into home four hours after we had left the crash pad, Abby's tail wagged wildly as soon as she spotted my husband. Happily coming up the steps inside, probably smelling us both there and finding her favorite toy on the rug, she settled right into her new home, tail wagging furiously.

It's good to have a Lab in the house again, trying out every single comfy place to lie down. I can almost hear Barkley up above saying: "Way to go, Agent Canine C-4, way to go!"

51

Finding Home

The night is cold. I dream of a windswept farm field covered in snow. In my dream, a form I could recognize yet not touch—fire in his hair, fire in his eyes. Speaking to me though I could not hear, mouth moving as if to taste—and I wake up. For a moment I don't know where I am, then I look around, smile and go back to sleep.

When I wake again the neighborhood is hushed. I'm not sure what time it is, as I don't have a clock on the wall or wear a wristwatch. I have an antique clock left to me by my mother, given to me not so that I remember time, for hers was short, but to forget it. Forget it as I move out into the world, gathering the wind to propel my journey, not holding my breath to conquer it; the folly of many a philosopher and fool.

The household is quiet. Abby the rescue Lab is snoozing in a patch of sunlight somewhere, dreaming the dreams of solar-powered dogs. I have a few hours off this morning before a long journey. The road will come soon enough; for now I can just enjoy the house, some writing, some coffee. Outside, the yard is perfect with the stillness of dew, the sun glinting between low branches. No dog tracks yet, no human or squirrel tracks; only a line of old trees standing with the enduring and ageless patience of static stillness, waiting for something. Perhaps they simply wait for me to venture out into the burgeoning chill of a not-quite-fall morning.

The neighborhood slumbering, I look out; innumerable shadows on the ground, as still as if they had been laid down upon it as stencils. Sunlight just a pencil tracing, drawing dark and light. The morning is here, now. Where I came from last night is only a distant memory.

Back behind the trees the sound of a train dies away to the click of a watch that is not there, running through another day somewhere far away for now, fire in his eyes, fire in his hair. The sound hangs in the air like punctuation, the clouds curled up above in small catnaps of infinity—only my small form, and perhaps a camera, to capture them. The train moves away in unshaken pull and balance, consuming inertia itself; its desire only a breath of steam in the cold air.

The light is soft, a cold blue fragility that speaks of shattered thought. Not quite enough light yet for photos, no tangible remembrance of the feeling; only words that gather up their own steam even as they fade away into silence.

The morning reminds me of one out in the woods long ago at a friend's farm.

―⊶⊷―

We had been setting out to check on an old tree blind before whitetail deer activity started. It had been some time since we'd visited, since I'd made my way out there. The woods looked ancient; evergreen trees bearing their load of snow on sagging shoulders, a few trees holding on to threadbare leaves gathered around their branches like a shawl. It had been an early snow, masking all the normal markings I would have used to find my way back to the house. As I went deeper into the woods I broke off a few small branches, small signs that I was on the right path, even as whole trees had fallen over trails I used to take.

From above a hawk dove down, rending the sky like faded blue cloth, its tattered remnants flung behind as he swooped down in search of something he needed to sustain. I'd not have seen him had I not remained totally still; his dive a brief blur, a mote from God's eye falling from heaven.

The old deer blind was still there and secure, so I began the journey back, looking carefully to make sure I was on the right path to light and safety. From a distance I could see the warm glow of the house. From the trees I heard the gentle huff of a buck—a greeting, a warning, his breath clouding the air in anticipation of that which he knows he wants. I caught only a glimpse of rack, its width indicating he had survived numerous hunts. He watched me, a Trojan with time and patience and the occasional Browning 20-gauge on her side.

On this day, though, the deer had nothing to fear from me—the dance between man and nature, the slow waltz of blood and need, stilled within me for now. That day, he and I were simply part of this same forest, one with the land. Though by my intellect and God's grace I had dominion over him, I would tender my stewardship carefully and leave him in peace. The recognition of freedom, the desire for life—full, rich, and red—was as conscious in me as in him, and is always there even when my higher nature slumbers. It courses through this earth and each of us, a deep red vein awaiting the divining rod of recognition.

He turned with a flick of a white tail and disappeared into the shadows, deeper into hundred-year-old woods. I wished I'd had a camera to capture that, to capture all that I can't see and can't remember later; so much here beyond the grasp of anything born or invented. Perhaps I could find words for it, if only silently; the apotheosis of our need voicing a thousand avatars.

—⚬⚬⚬—

Another evening, another stand of trees, the ones that line the driveway at home. Even as I'll roll in after traveling across several states this week, the path will be clear, the way familiar. As is often the case on arrival, I will be tired and hungry, anxious for the warmth of home and a little supper. Coming up past the house, those large pine trees brush up against the truck as I'll drive in, back deep behind the building.

The back of the property by the shop is quite dark; for a

moment I'll hesitate with the darkness and my weariness, not sure which way to turn. Then I'll notice the bent branch from my truck as I came in marking my path. I grab my bag even as I hear a familiar greeting, his breath clouding the air.

Gear is left in the enclosed porch, the black bag brought into the house for now. A black Lab comes in with a rush of air, her tail a baton against the music that now plays from somewhere within. The ancient gas stove fires its evening gun as dinner is prepared and consumed with thankful prayer.

Once again the neighborhood is hushed, hundred-year-old wood framing the room. From within comes a soft playful bark, the sound of voices; a blended murmur fading as a door softly closes. Inside a small wooden drawer an antique watch ticks without sound.

Tonight, a cup of coffee and the sound of an instrument playing soft music bring it all back in small ways as I gather those I love near me in spirit and thought; the smell of good coffee awakening something in me. I was hoping for snow, though it's still only late Fall; but it was not to be. The day dawned gray, the sky the color and texture of iron that quietly pressed down upon the land until it lifted up into the darkness without notice.

For I am home, surrounded by those that are my pack. Some in person and some in spirit; connected by a phone, a computer, an occasional hug. Not all of them family by blood but family all the same, with that same tangible connection, silent and invisible, like the draw of a bright flame that doesn't need immediate presence to warm you. Simple, loving human contact. Laughter with like minds and spirits. For being family is not simply about being home to a childhood memory that for me and many others does not exist anymore. It's not about whom or what have at your table but what you have in your heart. It's more than the faith that you actively practice or the faith that sits in quiet silence, waiting. It's something else: a connection to our friends and children, to the one who quietly loves us, to our God who gave us a wonderful gift. It's a visceral reminder that we are all connected, we are all worthy of love even as we sometimes have to release it.

Tonight as the light seeps out the sky—my future not what I'd planned on years ago, my family changed in ways we didn't expect quite yet—a momentary longing of homesickness wells up in me and threatens to spill over. I just stop, and for a moment my world is still. I look at the photos around me, the gifts from friends and family, the wagging tail of a dog we saved from certain death; the photo of a beautiful young redhead, my little Grace, now known as Rebecca, a mother of two beautiful girls. I look out onto the frost twinkling on the ground like tiny lights in the sun and breathe in deep the beautiful world around me; and my homesickness disappears like tears melting into snowflakes.

I realize that, just as love is not a lover, our family is who we share this journey with, not who shares our last name. These journeys take us many places. It is said the best ones lead us toward home, toward shelter, toward safety. But the best ones of all, however long they may take, lead us gently back to ourselves.

52

Unexpected Gifts

As I sorted through boxes brought from Dad's—some of my things, some of my late brother Allen's—I stifled a yawn.

I had rolled in quite late, followed by a long drive home, on the seat next to me a few Christmas presents I'd picked up during the week. Now they lie on the table with the mementos from my childhood Christmas. My husband is out of the country, so there is no rush to wrap the gifts before inquiring eyes spy the *Ronco Cap Snaffler Pocket Fisherman Dehydrator*. Next to his gifts is a mismatched and cheap little nativity set from my childhood home that I had packed and gotten through TSA (Baby Jesus not wanting to be mistaken for a liquid of more than three ounces and confiscated). The wise men are in pink and aqua and purple, riding shiny silver, humped, four-legged transports. (Pimp My Camel!) The rest of the scene, from another set obviously, is a small painted plaster Baby Jesus in an actual wooden manger.

On the TV, there is no good news. I'm exhausted to the point of dizziness. So I turn off the TV and turn on the Christmas lights.

They are there, strung on a sparse fake tree, known as the Rogaine Pine. It's not quite the Charlie Brown Tree, but it is close. But it's old and it's mine, strung with a few ornaments saved from childhood.

That night, after the TV goes silent and I'd been awake almost twenty hours, I just sit and look at the blank screen. The other lights are off. My sidearm lies on the table, free from its duty as well; a small dram of single malt in my hand; and an empty spot there on the couch here my black Lab Barkley used to lie; Miss Abby the Lab on the rug next to it.

As kids, Allen and I were quite inquisitive as to what was under the tree. When we were really small, we were told to leave the presents alone, no shaking, peeking, or such. We mostly obeyed. Though one year Mom sprayed the tree with that white flocking stuff popular in the '60s and '70s. We were innocently playing on the floor with our toy tanks and GI Joes, a flurry of motion that in children and bad generals is often used in lieu of a plan, when Mom walked in.

"Have you been under the tree?"

"No, Mom" we'd proclaim, feeling guilty even as the words came out of our mouths.

I still have the picture somewhere of the two of us there, our red hair covered in flocking, like a dusting of powdered sugar. *Busted!*

As we got older, we were allowed to check out the gifts under the tree, but only because Mom and Dad booby trapped the packages. With rocks, marbles, and all manner of things that made odd noises or gave the boxes odd shapes. We never could figure out what was in them, and our folks had much fun setting us up.

One never knows what is in that gift. What at first may seem to be without value, may become your most prized possession.

Sometimes the best gifts are the least expected ones. Christmas for us was not a flurry of dozens and dozens of gifts, the kids tearing into them like sharks, tossing one new toy aside with barely a glance and without a thank you for the next. In our home, each gift was savored, opened deliberately, because we knew that with our family's budget there would be only a few; and we wished to savor every moment of the unveiling.

But it did not prevent us from wanting those big and shiny expensive toys that we were likely not to get. Our bikes were used, carefully picked up by Dad and refurbished; my clothes were handmade, or hand-me-downs from my cousin Liz, two years older and about my build. But having such useful warm things didn't stop us from coveting something beyond our reach; the wanting so intense that even if we had received it, it would never have satisfied that picture we built of it there in that span between desire and possession.

But in the remembering—the coloring of the past by sound, movement, shape, and taste—I am thankful. Because my parents didn't buy us everything we wanted, for then we never would have appreciated what we had. And what we had was good. I remember a dollhouse that Dad spent hours toiling in the night assembling long after we were asleep. There was a chemistry set that didn't just look colorful like the ones now, but would actually blow things up if you were stupid. There were balls and Frisbees; and one year, two skimboards to take to the ocean, where I first learned to fly at ground level.

We go into adulthood with that iron and simple framework of the future we think will never betray us, as long as we continue to hope and to dare. Then life happens: we put our trust in the wrong people, we make choices we were raised not to make—and for a brief time that hope abandons us, leaving us only with the capacity still to dare.

Subsequent Christmases brought their own memories, as they do for many of us; some good, some painful. After such times it's easy to think we are no longer capable of hoping, only of daring. Until one day you realize that for every Christmas there was only the solitude, the privacy you once coveted that you now found has become the most complete privacy of all—the solitude in which every man is born, and in which every man will die.

It is then you realize, there as the snow falls outside and your single shadow creeps eastward, lengthening, that the gift of Christmas isn't what society wants you to believe. It's not someone under the mistletoe; it's not presents and shiny gold. It's the season of hope, even among chaos and darkness. For the world, for us, there is a gift that is the true reason the day is celebrated, there in the birth of a baby.

I glance at the cheap little plastic nativity scene and smile as I put the gifts aside to make a loaf of bread to rise as I sleep; hands working rhythmically, bringing with it that peacefulness that is like watching machinery in motion. I'll work as I wait for a call from the other side of the world. In that call, in that connection, there lies here and now every good memory ever made, even if the form of them all is mostly dust.

We can't change our work schedules; we can't change how people treat us. We can't always have everything we want, be it a new bike, good health, or a child. We can only prepare, dare, and continue to hope.

53

Bare Bones

Before this fire of sense decay,
This smoke of thought blow clean away,
And leave with ancient night alone
The stedfast and enduring bone.

—*The Immortal Part*, A. E. Housman

I woke at about 3:30 a.m. and entered the bathroom, only to be confronted by what was either a giant gnat or a drone. In either event, I dispatched it with a size seven moose slipper and crawled back into bed and tried to go back to sleep. Being on call always wears me out. I put in a full day at work, but I might also get called out in the middle of the night, so I get to bed extra early and then wake up in the middle of the night.

This is not good for the waistline or any sort of regular social plans with my husband, but it's a rhythm as familiar to me as the sound of wheels hitting a runway.

It's hard to believe that twenty years have gone since that frightened young woman drove through the night to start a new life after her last one imploded. Twenty years in which she got to meet her daughter, raise a good dog, reconnect with her family, and remarry, so very happily. Twenty years in which she gathered around her those that are now her family, including so many not related by blood or marriage, only friendships rooted deep in the Midwest soil.

There's a band of severe weather up north right now, creeping on down as if it's slow enough we won't notice. I hope the phone doesn't ring tonight. If I'm lucky, it will just be heavy rain and I won't be standing outside somewhere looking like a five foot eight lightning pole. I have a mental picture of how *that* might turn out and think of a sign on a restaurant wall in St. Petersburg that said: *Parachute for sale, never opened, used once, small stain.*

It looks like thunderstorms are building, but I will hope for only rain.

Rain I'm familiar with, the family having left Montana but for a summer home to move out near the Washington coast. I like the rain. The rain washes clean, but it also leaves its mark. Gouges from rivulets in the calloused summer soil as if scraped by hard nails. Bullet strikes in the hard earth. Marks that will not fade until further rain falls, warm spring rain that nourishes and renews.

Just as my first spring here in the Midwest was a revelation, my first winter was an eye opener despite being from a Montana family. Dense fogs of ice crystals that coated everything;

thundersnow; winds that would blow off the prairie from the West and rampaging clippers that came down from Alberta, bearing with them not a friendly greeting, but rather a sudden sharp slap in the face.

It's a cold blowing truth that there's something within all of us that can be gathered up, strengthened. Something commanding that can change the form of a life. The weather brings components of force, some deep innate working in our souls. Lightning cleaves the sky as a machete, the smell of cordite in the air lingering like gunpowder. Thunder echoing as a brace of artillery booming under a gunmetal sky; the power of the sky a transcendent weapon that can form or scar, however we view it, the landscape of our world.

Sometimes one has to work outside in it, bundled up in farm wear or arctic military gear. You do what you need to while the wind laments, whispering of darkness in the earth. Your own voice, the sound of another voice in your ear evocative of evenings of past warmth compel you forward; for to stop moving out here is to freeze to death.

I delivered my first calf in the cold; the calf not budging from his mother's womb, the mother not helping in any fashion for reasons known only to her. There was no easy way to do this but to go in and help position the calf, hoping I wouldn't get a broken arm from the contractions for my efforts. There, the head—my fingers finding the mouth; the feel of the unborn tongue, there tasting, life and breath and air in my fingers. There is nothing in the world lonelier than being there for the

birth of a solitary creature or the death of one. A little reposi-
tioning, a good push from mama, the spreading of bone—and
he was out, protesting heartily as outside thunder flashed, illuminating sweat and blood and, for this night at least, new life.

It is a wonder to me how that bone spreads for birth; yet when
I see those telltale marks upon the bones in human remains—
those marks on the dorsal side on the pubic symphysis near the
margins of the articular surfaces and in the preauricular groove
or sulci of the ilia—to my eyes they aren't notches of childbirth, they are the scars of sacrifice to save just one solitary life.

I stayed in that place, in the shadow of that barn, until the
house was empty and the land grew blood: looking in the mirror one day, motionless, eyes downcast, looking as if I was waiting for that blow I'd already received.

It was time to move on—back to graduate school, back to
myself.

Someone close to me asked why I was fascinated with the science of bones. I didn't answer him at the time, but I will now.
I have studied bones untouched by anything but time. I have
studied bones in fragments, commingled with so many others,
burned and broken and laid bare to the elements. Still, I am
always fascinated by the strength of that which is unfleshed.
Bones are what lies at the center of us—not the heart, but that
part of us that is the last thing to ever be dissolved even if cut
or disassembled or burned. It is the hardest, strongest, most
unwavering part of us; that which supports us, the last piece of

us that remains of this earth when everything else is lost; the surviving remnant of all that was dear to us.

But even the strongest of bone can be broken under the fragility of human flesh, as fate resolves us of all integrity, leaving us wrenched asunder of all that was. Smells of cooling flesh and salty tears, illusions of ice and rain and fire, detached and secret, yet oh-so-familiar. How easy when we are so very young to think we are invincible, that our choices are the right ones.

Certainly some of my adventures would indicate that I too subscribed to such moments. But with adulthood not only comes responsibility, but awareness. Suddenly, for myriads of reasons—aging, fear, illness, the evil intent of man—the people around you, as reliable as the sunrise, can without warning leave you. In their absence the sound of their goodbyes resonates in the emptying heart of your soul. You hear it always, but you do not respond to that fading sound, for to do so would be to admit to your own mortality.

But I hear the echo. I see it in the shape and form of things broken past integrity. I see it in a stormy sky, as lightning stains the dark, bitter air shaping the earth in cold darkness. I see it walking the landscape as the earth warms anew the sky, blind and warm upon me, touching my skin, my form a wet seed growing wild in the cold, dark earth.

I think of that as my cell phone pushes against bone when the truck hits a bump as I'm driving under a night as deep and black as the river Styx. It's on my hip as I drive miles through county after county, past fields waiting to be planted and later, fields of hay; totems of silos huddled like Iroquois lodges standing solitary and watching. Somewhere out here tonight will be the truth—when nature and fate poured forth its fury, spilling liquid, scorching earth.

As I drive I watch the sky for massing clouds, the vertebrates of highway passing underneath, the soft thump of tires as they pass over those small ridges of calcified earth and asphalt bone. I touch a small nail that dangles from the dashboard along with a small piece of animal bone, found in the woods one day. That piece of bone is a comfort to me, like this landscape— hard and practical, yet capable of great strength and the flexibility to withstand what the heavens can throw at it. So strong and delicate, the bones of man and Earth.

Later, I stand in a field, placing small flags to mark what my eye has captured. The wind picks up, swirling around the dust of spent lusts and ancient lies. Ghosts of sad reflection, a hundred thoughts never formed and a thousand words never uttered. The wind sweeping my head of any emotion other than the task at hand, until the very roar of it is a warning to look up. When I do, when I truly look at the sky, I know in a moment when I can safely cast my eyes back down or run for shelter. It's like listening in an ancient church to a priest chanting in a tongue which I do not even need to know to comprehend. They are words that belong in the defensive perception of light and order which is our safety.

I put my tools back into the soil leaving my own parturition scar, trying to save a life by its closure, even if it's mine. I keep one eye on the horizon even as I return to work. Whatever you do, don't blink.

You watch, you prepare; and sometimes, like other things in life, it sneaks up on you. One moment calm and upright, the next flashes of light against the sky—wheels running hard and fast either toward the storm or away. Previously dying leaves blown into fence rows, coming back to life with movement. The sky comes hungering after the land like a hungry wolf, something struggling for life between the two while pulled and tossed with need; something flaring up—as old as time, as necessary as water.

You never know when the wind will come up, how it will touch you. You can arrive here as cold and hard and flat as the armor the land is laid with; and eventually the wind will arise, a murmuring voice that calls you in the night. Warm rain released like coins from above, falling like a gift; seeping in under your surface, leaving only a small telltale drops on your skin as the sky clears. You look at the table, there lying side by side a small stamped envelope with your name on it and some change, pennies from heaven indeed.

From outside comes the crack of thunder, the rain tattooing itself onto the roof as a truck door slams. From inside the house comes the soft bark of a gentle dog, nipping at the wind like the rain itself.

54

Strays

Our friends Mr. B. and MC have a half dozen cats at their country home, all of whom I believe were dumped out there by the unfeeling. All were found cold and extremely hungry. It's good to see them now: well-fed and happy, cared for as indoor-only cats in a spacious country home with a huge basement for them to explore. I remember evenings on the couch with Barkley, surrounded by the original four cats—their purrs of contentment as they lay on top of the cushions or next to him, drawing on the warmth of his big furry body while suffering the occasional snoot with a clawless and gentle swat to his nose.

These cats are like family, but I am a dog person even as I have a soft spot for any animal that is homeless or mistreated. Walking through my neighborhood with Abby yesterday I saw a cat, arrested within the eyes of a dog, back pulled up high in the apostrophe of fear as she held poised for fight or flight. I pulled Abby gently away; she had had cats at her foster Mom's house so we weren't in for a rumble. But I didn't want Abby to get a clawed nose for her curiosity. The cat's coat was in good condition as far as I could tell, but it was thin, likely a stray. I was going to see where she went, where she might have a home; but the cat was gone in a flash before I could check on her well-being. I'd seen her before, always hanging around the same spot in the fence where she likely had found a safe place to sleep.

We see them on the streets, in shelters; the fortunate ones collected by rescue groups, the unfortunate—the look in their eyes heartrending. But animals aren't the only strays we see, people fall into that same category. I'm not talking about the homeless, necessarily, but those people that by circumstance or transplant find themselves in a new city: for a new job or a fresh start where they don't know anyone; or they are stranded somewhere while traveling for a day or more due to weather and fate.

I found myself in that circumstance the year I moved to a new state to take a promotion opportunity. I'd only been on that job a few weeks, not enough time to make any friends. I'd moved here from back east, too far to visit any old friends after the cost of the move. My parents were in San Diego at my step aunt's condo, where they spent every Thanksgiving and Christmas after Dad remarried. I wasn't invited—the place simply not being big enough for the whole blended family. Dad felt badly that I'd be alone, but he wanted his wife to be happy, her time with her sister growing short and the rest of her siblings gone. I understood that and would visit them for a belated Christmas at home on their return; but it still made the holiday lonely.

I remember walking out to my little car from my workplace the night before Thanksgiving that first year there, as the sky spat cold rain and I felt a tear on my face. I'm not sure why; as a professional pilot in my younger days I'd spent many a holiday alone on call or in a hotel. Years later holidays were busy times at work. But that night it sort of got to me—I really had no place to go but home to Barkley and a sandwich, my kitchen torn up for remodeling. I was hoping someone leaving when I did would remember that I had no family near and swing back by to ask me to join them for dinner the next day.

As I walked to the car I saw a gleam out of the corner of my eye in the darkness, a movement; and I smiled thinking someone remembered me and was turning back with an invitation. But it was nothing more than an illusion, that faint glimpse of reflection imagined there as you gaze into the depths of a wishing well, only to find cold stillness. There was no car, just a flash of light reflected off a nearby road—and it brought back every bad moment as a child: those moments we have all had when we feared we just didn't fit in, that we didn't belong.

I was always the one inviting the new kid to play with us, befriending the nerdy and the odd. Perhaps it was because I viewed myself that way. So when I was a very young flight instructor, living out of a suitcase with no roots, I decided to continue that tradition and share my table with others like me. With most of us on call to give an introductory flight to a prospective student, hoping to earn some dollars to pay next quarters tuition or too broke to fly home commercially, many of us had no place to go on Thanksgiving day. So I hung up a flier on the instructor's bulletin board at my airport, for my coworkers and any errant corporate pilot in the area. An invitation to come over to my little place for Thanksgiving dinner.

I'd not say I was friends with all these guys from the perspective that we would continue to hang out together when we finished college, going off to fly for the military or the airlines. These were simply people I'd spent hours in the cockpit with getting my various instructor ratings; occasionally getting the %*#@ scared out of us; absorbing the wonderful colors and shapes and shadows of the sky; making temporary homes in a series of small apartments with multiple roommates; cramming as much as possible into the rare twenty-four hours we actually were off with a light study load. So yes, we were family, if only related by adventure and empty pockets. And for that I could think of no better reason than to peel thirty pounds of potatoes, bake five pies, and go to bat my big green eyes at the butcher to talk him out of that extra ham at half-off.

Yes, thirty pounds of potatoes; for although I expected RSVPs from about six people, I ended up with twenty-seven. Pilots I worked with; a couple of our mechanics; and corporate pilots that used our facility and stayed at the local hotel while their passengers enjoyed Thanksgiving with family. Everyone arrived with drinks and chips and, thankfully, some extra rolls and a couple of pies from the grocery store.

It was a wonderful evening with massive quantities of food consumed, countless stories told, and much laughter; eating until we couldn't eat any more. There was something starry in the kitchen that night, where I learned as much about my ability to plan and organize as I did about the essential bond that a meal around the table creates—even if it's only a bunch of card tables shoved together with white bleached sheets over them.

Did it mean that we all got along perfectly after that night? No, for there were still those days that intruded darkly on hours normally full of light. Those long, close-quartered days where we plowed through thick dark clouds to reach ice-covered firmament, cursing the weather and long lines for takeoff. Days where the alarm clock snatched us violently out of wrung-out sleep, sweeping us all back into the thrall, impotent for days against returning to home; knowing that instead of getting a nap afterwards most of most of us would be heading off to night classes. As much fun as flying could be, after a few months of such a schedule even the best of us got a little self-absorbed. Add in constant travel, books, and study hall, and it was a life of scattered adrenalin, little sleep, and scant time for real relationships. Just like life for many of us now, with families and jobs and pets and demands.

But that night, if only for a few hours, we had that bond of family and food, warmth and safety. It was that moment when chance aligns with time whose only foe is death; and together, death's darkness seemed so very far away.

Strays.

You see them at any airport. The frazzled traveler who just missed the last flight; that young student or soldier sleeping on the floor after their flight got canceled, without the means to secure a hotel room. I've offered a hot coffee and a sandwich with a smile to more than one of those people I saw stranded at the airport. Why? Because I have been that young person with rumbling stomach, surrounded by strangers, wanting only to be home.

I had a flight between two Midwest cities a few years back, after I'd picked up a couple of days work as a contract corporate pilot. The city where was going to fly wasn't home, but it was near where I was spending Thanksgiving with friends. I got the call to cover for a pilot out sick for a company I'd done some contract work before. Easy money; and the holiday weekend was just about over anyway.

The sky was cold and cloudy as I waited for my return flight to be followed by a long drive home, but there was no precipitation. All of a sudden our flight was canceled with no reason given; we were only told we'd be on another flight really soon. I didn't see any mechanics at the plane and the flight crew was all there, so I called Flight Service for the aviation weather, giving them the registration number of the plane I'd just flown in the previous night. They said there was severe icing aloft, unusual to be so widespread, but deadly. No one big or small was going to be flying out of that airport most likely for the rest of the day.

At this point we were standing in line to be rebooked, the word not having gotten to the gate that the airport would essentially be shutting down all flights. There was a well-dressed gentleman behind me. We had chatted a bit and it turned out his wife worked at the same bank one of the folks I had spent the holiday with. I quietly told him about the weather and explained that *no one* was going to be flying and I was going to get a rental car *now* as the flight was just a "hop," and getting home back to where my car was parked was just a three and a half hour drive. A couple other people overheard. I asked, "Do you want to go with me?" With a quiet nod, four of us snuck out of the line. For it only takes word that the last flights are canceling to start a disturbed hum in the customer service line, like bees—before they move in an agitated swarm to the rental car counters, with stinging glances to the priority customers, the worker bees hoping for one solitary economy car to be left. I wanted to get out before *that* happened.

The weather out of the clouds was great, just a little snow. We made the trip in four hours, everyone calling their spouses or friends to say that they would be a bit late and whether they needed a ride from the airport. On the drive we were strangers, and we weren't. We talked of holiday plans, kids, and vacations when it got warm. There were bad puns and way too many references to the movie *Trains, Planes and Automobiles*—something only folks who saw that movie would appreciate. "You're going the wrong way!" one of us exclaimed—and the whole car erupted in laughter like we were a bunch of grade school kids, the cool kids. "Those aren't pillows!" as we laughed again, just having fun with no fears of rejection or hurt or loss.

With a stop for sandwiches at one of the toll plazas, we soon made it—only to find the terminal pretty much deserted, most of the inbound flights coming from north or east also canceled. My traveling companions thanked me for having made that call and offering to pay for the rental car. I had let them pay for gas, and that's all I wanted.

We said our goodbyes and walked away toward home. The Sun, whose brilliant form dwarfs us all into the smallest of particles upon the Earth as we are held within its glare, was hidden behind the steeled gray of cloud cover. With its brightness now captured behind stratified doors, the night fell upon us as we walked to our cars; and it was as if we were all just shadows, covered with a fine, soft scattering of night like ash.

I never saw any of them again.

Thanksgiving for me this year was one of those "sandwich days," not for lack of an invitation with friends but personal and work related. Still, it gave me time to think and reflect, something that is as important as giving thanks. The human heart is large enough to contain the entire world, and it's small enough to be felled by just one being. Yet it is valiant enough to bear all burdens when you realize you are not alone.

As the phone rang with the cherished voice of my husband letting me know he had reached his destination safely, I realized I had much to be thankful for. Even in an empty house there was a gentle snore of a contented rescue Lab, until the clock struck the duty hour and I gathered a black bag and gear in case the phone rang in the middle of the night. But before that happened there was something I needed to do. With a quick warm hand pressed for a moment on top of a cold square box in which my furry best friend lay, I left the house and walked to a little drug store a block away, a can opener and a little plastic bowl in my pocket. I got a can of cat food and put it out in a bowl along a solitary fence.

For at one time, everyone is a stray.

55

Goodbye

They say the veil between this world and the next is a thin one. I don't consciously think of it all the time; but there are moments when all is falling apart around me, tears getting the best of me, and my mind goes upward. In those moments I wonder if Mom, Allen, and Barkley are looking down on me. In those moments the veil is rendered with one cutting edge of a scalpel, a clean bloodless cut, as if the blade severed not flesh but a sob; restoring this small place, this moment, to peace.

Sometimes it takes a while after a loss to get to that quiet spot. For it is not just the battlefield that has to be conquered, but the silence that remains when the field is cleared—that silence in which the person left behind has time to remember; and in that mute aftermath make the decision to move forward knowing their only guide may be a heavenly one.

I'd like to think it's that heavenly presence watching from above that restores me, not the thought of a long hot bath when I get home or the Midol kicking in. On such occasions I say a quiet prayer of thanks and hope that Mom didn't see what mayhem erupted when I attempted to make her cereal-pretzel-nut party mix recipe in a seventy-year-old gas oven after three glasses of wine.

As kids we figured Mom always had eyes in the back of her head; and there wasn't much we got away with, always feeling that vast weight of her watching. Though my brother is probably glad she never got wind of the "live possum in the bathroom at school" incident. The possum wasn't harmed, but several teachers armed with metal garbage pails to capture it were *less* than pleased.

We tried to behave, for we learned early that the punishment was often swift and appropriate; none of this "Oh, you're having a tantrum, let me buy you that toy" that too often seems to pass for parenting today. But we were kids. I still recall the story where Allen, three years old or so, dropped dirt in the open can of paint for the new house as he apparently didn't like the original color, preferring brown instead. And if you open the bathroom drawer at Dad's you can still see the swirls of Mom's red lipstick where I decided to do a little "drawing." Still, in our adventures and misadventures, Allen was my best friend.

I remember Allen letting me tag along his paper route, not being ashamed of his little sister as most of his friends would have been, but teaching me the perfect curve ball of paper onto a porch. I remember road trips where we would playfully bicker and play with toy soldiers in the back of the car. Mine in my chubby little hands, his more grown and nimble. He'd move to my side of the station wagon seat with his troops, setting camp until I yelled "MOM!" and we'd be told to be quiet for at least fifteen minutes. We'd sit in perfect stoic silence, shooting looks back and forth at each other as if dueling with foils while we plotted, planned, and waited for the laughter to burst out because we just couldn't hold it in.

I remember evenings in a 1960s kitchen. Mom washed the dishes as Allen would bring in that last platter in from the dining room. Dad would be having a cup of coffee after dinner, and then he would make sure the knives were sharpened and put away, the dishes dried. Dinner was steelhead trout caught by Dad himself, there on a tireless morning of gossamer threads and mist.

There would be much talking, the sound a steady hum interspersed with the metallic clink of utensils together like small machinery working away. Outside it was dark; there was a war ongoing somewhere, there was crime, there was evil. It's all out there somewhere, as is the darkness—pressing against the house like water does a dam. Not with obvious movement, just that steady pressure that is the desire to break through. But inside, as children we did not sense it; for us there was only the light that seeped outward through the cracks between the curtains. So much of it here that it could be shared with the darkness.

I remember all the Sundays we went to church, even those earliest memories of service on Easter Sunday. I'd sit as still and as tall as I could, but I could only see the backs of heads. When I was really little, Mom would give me a tiny little bag of Cheerios, so if I got hungry and fidgety I could eat a few, one at a time. My feet hurt and my new dress itched, but I knew mostly to behave, acting up only earning me a brisk march outside for a swat on the bottom, while Jesus looked down from the wall in the vestibule with an expression that said: "You shouldn't lob a Cheerio at your brother."

Easter Sunday traditions rarely varied: we'd get up to find a small basket outside our bedroom door containing jelly beans and candy; and for me one early Easter, a stuffed bunny. Oh, how I loved that bunny, dragging it around everywhere. Mom occasionally had to wash it and hung it up on the clothesline by its ears to dry. Over time most of his fur was worn away, he lost his plastic eyes, his nose fell off, and his ears were beyond floppy. But I still loved him, keeping him even into adulthood even if I couldn't always keep him safe from harm.

I didn't much like the early hour or wearing a dress on those Easter Sundays. But even to a child there was something magical about the music, the organ straining with the sonorous tone of a parent while the choir, voices freed from parental caution to play quietly, rose up in a flurry of joy—heartfelt in their gathering volume, assuming the shapes of angels to my small form below. I'd actually sit still for that as their voices faded away into the still air, as clear and delicate as struck glass.

After that it was Sunday as usual. Normally our folks made Sunday a family day of board games and books and music; but as hyped up on Easter candy sugar as we were, Mom was willing to forgo that to let us run off a little steam. So we donned our cowboy holsters and six-shooters and headed out. Allen would get out the door first and point his squirt gun at me with a stern, "You'd best get out here, you lily-livered coward," to which I simply stuck my tongue out at him through the screen. It tasted like dirt.

He didn't look at all scared.

But somehow the play always evolved into us being on the same side even if all we had to be the "bad guy" was the neighbor's cat or a menacing shrub. I took more than one "bullet" for my big brother, even if I could barely keep up with him on my little legs. More than one knee was bloodied in my battle to save him—the scabs becoming a Bactine-infused mark of my sacrifice.

But it's hard for kids as they grow up to keep the cohesion we had living in the same house. We are bound together by family, but often scattered by distance; dealing with our own tragedies, things much worse than a failed model contest, keeping it in and not saying much. But inevitably we did grow up, Allen leaving for submarine service when I was still in school.

I missed him. I remember walking in the woods with compass and pocket knife and seeing an elk crash into flight from a stand of small trees off in the distance, the sound seemingly curving around the whole earth. I couldn't move, frozen by the sound. I simply stood, open-mouthed, incredulous as to how big the elk really was close-up and all the thoughts flowing through my head, turning to follow his now invisible running. For lack of any other response to his leaving, I picked up a rock and threw it hard and deep into the forest in which he ran, the stone glinting like a knife, disappearing into the last copper ray of sun before it dipped behind the trees.

"I don't want you to go," was all I could say as I stood there in the fading light, feeling very small and alone.

But my big brother came back; Allen always came back. And he'd call me when he could and I'd tell him about school and my misadventures in physics, both in and out of the classroom, and we'd laugh. We both always laughed easily and well. We didn't worry about politics, budgets, deadlines, or knowing that sometimes keeping your mouth shut had to be the better part of valor. Even as I entered adulthood, we could still laugh and say, "It's five o clock somewhere," as I raised my first glass of amber liquid in a toast to endless oceans and skies. It was a golden time, one in which we hadn't fully learned to look at everything in a critical eye of war or loss.

When Allen got married, I was there at his wedding near the Naval base in California, wearing a lime green bridesmaid dress with a turtleneck that I would not have worn for the Pope, the Queen of England, or Marshall Dillon. (Though given how Miss Kitty dressed, Marshall Dillon would have liked it.) But I wore it for Allen.

Soon he and I were both grown, no longer to have imaginary gun battles with toy pistols. But he knew as I did that either of us would give our life for the other.

Though those early gun battles among siblings and friends were only child's play, they will be played out years later for many of us. For there will come times of fighting, of blood and prayer, of plunges into the deepest waters and ascents into unknown skies. Moments where we approach nearest of all to God, just as on Sunday we drew nearer to him, there in the peace and the fury that is both the promise and end of all faith.

With Allen no longer living under the same roof but always looking out after me, we charged ahead—mindful only of our duty to protect and to uphold, minds and hearts purged then of sins that lay behind. Summed and absolved by the formal fury of a minister's intonation from the pulpit; moving forward, sacrificing ourselves as need be so that somewhere, someone could live for a little while beneath the safe, warm exhalation of faith and trust.

But overall, I don't think we gave our parents too much grief even as they worried about us, Allen under the seas as I was up in the skies somewhere.

Then as our parents aged, the tides were turned. Be it my step-mom's Alzheimer's or simply nearing a hundred years on this planet, there was a lot on our plates the last few years in taking care of Dad. After my stepmom passed it got a little easier, though there was still a lot to do to assist him. But I always had my brother to carry a big part of that load. When Allen moved in with Dad all he wanted to do was make our dad's life easier, telling me he hoped Dad would live to be 115. Though quietly, he just wanted to outlive Dad, to lessen that burden of grief on the man who was his hero and his family. Unfortunately, Allen lost that bet, leaving Dad alone, and keeping the fact from him that his cancer was stage IV when first diagnosed, though I knew that the treatment would only buy some time, not a cure.

I flew back and forth as often as I could during that time, using vacation, sick leave, and long weekends to see them, my budget no longer "can I get a new car this year?," but rather "Is there enough in checking for another airline ticket and rental car on top of the nursing assistance?" Married only months, my husband would travel with me when he could, to make the repairs and such to keep the house functioning. My dad loves him and is happy I married an engineer, not that longhaired kid with the red Mustang and electric guitar he would *not* let me date in high school. When I couldn't be there, Allen's two grown kids and my cousin Liz would take Dad on little outings, wrapping up as many memories they could on those short weekends.

Dad is welcome to live with any of us in the family, but he refuses, not willing to leave that house in which he outlived two beloved wives and his firstborn daughter. I understand. I was raised in that house after they adopted Allen and me, not to replace that child that they lost, but simply to find an outlet for the love they held so deeply.

The house hasn't changed much, fresh paint, new flowers. The marks of children raised here after they had left Montana; a small playhouse out back; the marks on a door where we grew and grew. On the table in the dining room where he and my brother last held hands to say grace, a photo of a pair of blue eyes in which his whole world achieved its value by the response he could draw from them. This was a woman who was completely necessary to him and will remain so even as her actual presence is but the sheen of an old sewing machine forever stilled, the rose petals in her garden long since gone to dust.

What I remember the most from those trips is some little scraps of blue paper. For on the door to Dad's house, after Allen got that death sentence he held in like breath until the end, there was a little clipboard on which he wrote a day's thoughts. Some of the things written would make sense only to us. Others were simply smiles, made with the little smiley bull face, as "Bull" was his nickname—he with the red hair and the seemingly unstoppable build. Fridays were always remembered, often with a big T.G.I.F. and exclamation points, for Allen lived for Fridays, when he could leave his job as a Navy contractor and drive down to visit his best friend from childhood, and spend time with Dad.

When I'd go home to visit there would be a note for me. Some were notes for friends. Allen might mention the rain or remind his country what is right as if it could read; but each day was an affirmation that life was being lived and hearts were being cared for. He never said anything about the cancer coming back in force, hiding the truth from Dad, though he couldn't from me—for he was dying and his days were dwindling. Still, each day there was that smiley bull face and a little note for whoever came to the door.

Allen had a long career in the submarine service. He had risked so much and so very quietly, yet his whole life was summed up in those small little moments in which he could care for the man who didn't have to be his dad. It was as if he was honing his life down to one moment, just as the mighty Chinook salmon concentrates its whole life down to that one last journey, that one last leap before relinquishing it.

Though Allen denied there was anything wrong, I knew—and I went and made another visit, just to spend some time with him. There was little resemblance to the photos of the handsome redheaded man in the Naval uniform. His once-red hair was gone, the beard, the round rosy cheeks that I might have suggested would have made for a good Santa Claus—if he didn't have dirt on me about the Arc Welder Incident—were sunken. Only his eyes looked the same, those light blue orbs which neither the defeat of years or this battle could dim. Picturing his gaunt form as he slept, it was as if all of him was evaporating; muscle and flesh like water vanishing until little remained but those deep blue pools. But what remained still saw with what pride upholds when the body fails, a frail hand held up briefly as he drifts to sleep, and a not-forgotten flag above a ravaged citadel.

We stayed up late on that last night, raising a glass of amber liquid and talking until Allen nodded off in the easy chair. Each time I didn't know if I'd hear his voice again, quietly saying as his eyes closed, "I don't want you to go." I had uttered those same words silently to someone else not long ago. Words quietly released in that quiet tone of slow amazement, as if I had not known until I uttered them the depths from which they came.

56

The Band Plays On

The last note was dated April 4, 2014.

It was a Friday, Allen's favorite day of the week as evidenced by all of these little notes on blue paper. But this one contained another note at the bottom and another little smile: a message from his daughter whom he would not see again. He died without warning exactly two weeks later, collapsing in the driveway after bringing Dad's trash bins up from the curb. It was Good Friday. He had to be carried into the house, a hundred pounds gone from his large frame, held up like a child, his feet remembering the earth, even as they no longer touched it.

Allen's last words to our dad were "Doctor." Dad tried to comfort him, telling him the doctor was there. My brother said, "No, *your* doctor, Dad, don't forget your appointment next Wednesday, it's important." His last words, his last thoughts only for the well-being of the man who raised us.

As I desperately tried to get to the airport to get a flight to see him, I physically felt him leave me. We'd been through foster care, adoption, the whole "Mom caught us taking the TV apart" incident, to an adult life spent serving our country—still as bonded as we were as small children, flung out to the wolves together before being saved. Minutes after I felt his leaving, a trembling in my chest like a released harp string, there and gone, the phone rang. It was Dad's next-door neighbor and friend, letting me know Allen had passed there in that minute I felt him. I could only lift one hand up from the steering wheel for a moment towards the sky, a toast in tears.

No regrets, no anger. From the very beginning we left it in God's hands, one way or the other. That time comes for all of us where we cease to be, where *is* becomes *was*, where those we love must weigh our empty body down under stone as what we *are* is lifted up to Heaven. That wooden box that calls for all of us is too small to catch all of the memory of courage and love; and so it spills out upon the ground to be gathered up like golden leaves. But that box is still big enough to be a shadow over what remains if we let it. As I looked at those little scraps of paper to be gathered up and brought home from Dad's, I remember a man who refused to stand under that shadow even as I struggled to feel him watching over me.

It wasn't until I brought this little clipboard home last week that I felt Allen so close. I had not felt that, not even as we collected up his things: a uniform; a little toy submarine that held office supplies; and the live flare gun found in his nightstand (I do *not* want to know why that was there). The sense of distance between us was profound.

After I placed it in my carry-on bag to come with me, I sat down by a side table where the piano once stood, the one Allen played first and then I, my always wanting to do what he did. As I sat, I tapped music upon it with my fingers as if it could respond. Things will change, as much as we wish them to remain, I thought to myself as I played a tune upon soundless wood— of ambered wine, the fall of autumn leaves, and goodbyes that are like sharpened knives.

That last night there was a quiet one, preparing a meal for Dad, getting trounced at cribbage, then doing the dishes as he went to sleep watching football.

Outside the darkness lapped at the house, but it wasn't truly dark here on the river; a bright light bobbed somewhere out on the water. It was more than a light for the river pilot, it was a beacon of safe harbor itself; and all that remained to him of a difficult journey was the shortening space between that brilliant light and his own motion forward.

As I finished up the dishes I kept my movements quiet so Dad could sleep undisturbed. In his dreams he is still a young man, setting up a home post-World War II with Mom, his high school sweetheart. Theirs was a town full of music and dreams and tall hills covered with ceaseless timber; the rain not a gray blanket but a sound, a rising and swelling with the gusts of emotion and passion that was worth waiting for. That place is still alive for him; threads of silken light unwinding from whirring spools, the sound of his children laughing in an old house near the water; in dreams of steelhead trout that never grow old, never tire.

We said our goodbyes the next day, never knowing if we'd see each other again. After landing back home, driving back with that little clipboard with the scraps of blue paper upon it, I finally felt my brother near me, over me, watching—a sailor never actually leaving his watch. It was a sad but comforting feeling, and I talked to Allen as I drove as if he could hear. I talked through the chartless latitude of my loss; and even in silence he comforted with a muted murmuring that was as soothing as the roar of an enduring sea.

When I pulled into the driveway my face was wet with tears, but I was *remembering*. So much to remember: my brother, my daughter, those small pieces of them I had, those pieces I can still hold onto even if I do not possess them.

From inside my house comes the clatter of the toenails of Abby the rescue dog on the hardwood floors as my husband opens the door. On the wall is a calendar my daughter Rebecca made me, with pictures of my two beautiful grandchildren—children that would not exist but for one scared, lonely teenager and one choice so many years ago. That choice, one that could only be made by one person, meant Rebecca had a chance at a childhood like I did; with two parents who loved her and had the means to provide for her a warm home and grace around a family table—the everlasting blessing of family.

From within my bag I draw out a small clipboard on which rest some scraps of blue paper. I hold it up as I get out of the vehicle, as an orchestra conductor holds up that slender baton that conveys within its weightless form all of the fierce fire and yearning and heartache that can be contained in one moment of history.

My husband takes it from me and holds me close as the music starts.

CPSIA information can be obtained at www.ICGtesting.com
Printed in the USA
LVOW08s1611300415

436756LV00002B/251/P